SPRINTER

SPRINTER

*The Life and Times of a
Professional Roadracer*

MALCOLM ELLIOTT
with JEFF CONNOR

PELHAM BOOKS
Stephen Greene Press

PELHAM BOOKS/Stephen Greene Press

Published by the Penguin Group
27 Wrights Lane, London W8 5TZ, England
Viking Penguin Inc., 40 West 23rd Street, New York, New York 10010, USA
The Stephen Greene Press Inc., 15 Muzzey Street, Lexington, Massachusetts 02173, USA

Penguin Books Australia Ltd., Ringwood, Victoria, Australia
Penguin Books Canada Ltd, 2801 John Street, Markham, Ontario, Canada L3R 1B4
Penguin Books (NZ) Ltd, 182-190 Wairau Road, Auckland 10, New Zealand

Penguin Books Ltd, Registered Offices: Harmondsworth, Middlesex, England

First published 1990

Typeset in Linotron, 11 on 13½pt Clearface Regular by Goodfellow and Egan, Cambridge
Made and printed in Great Britain by Butler and Tanner, Frome

A CIP catalogue record for this book is available from the British Library.

ISBN 0 7207 1939 9

Contents

Foreword
by Stephen Roche

The name of Malcolm Elliott was familiar to me long before I met him. I remember reading about his exploits in British events like the Sealink International and the Milk Race and realised then that here was a star in the making.

Eventually, of course, we became team-mates with Fagor and I knew that my judgement had not been wrong. As a sprinter, Malcolm is one of the fastest things on two wheels over the last 150 metres of a race, but he is also that rare thing – a sprinter who can get over hills and still remain very, very quick in a finish. He has tons of class.

Off the bike I have always found Malcolm a sensitive soul who likes nothing better than to relax with headphones, deep in his favourite music. I think there's a lot of feeling behind that quiet exterior.

Malcolm knows what he wants out of this cycling life and is prepared to go out and get it. I admire him for that and I admire his sheer ability. In spite of his achievements I always feel Malcolm could go a lot further if he was to live a bit more seriously and work harder. But then he seems to be getting by very well with his approach to life – and maybe if he was to change, that wouldn't be the real Malcolm Elliott!

Stephen Roche

1. Mister Big

The ski resort of La Plagne stands at 7,000 feet in the Haute Savoie of the French Alps, a conglomeration of pylons, purpose-built apartment blocks and hire shops. On the morning of 23 July 1987, I woke in the flats complex known as Residence Aime, 2,000 metres high on a hillside overlooking the village, and as I had done for the previous 20 days tried to work out where I was. The previous three weeks had passed in the haze of pain and discomfort and bewilderment that people call the Tour de France. My legs, body and mind ached and all I could do was curse the sadists who thought up the idea of race stages that end on the top of mountains. I looked forward to the finish in Paris four days ahead, a quick return to my home in Sheffield, South Yorkshire and relief from the battering I had taken since the first stage in West Berlin.

Nine riders under the trade team name of ANC Halfords had set out from Britain at the beginning of July that year to contest the greatest marathon in sport. By the time we got to La Plagne there were four survivors. At that moment I wished myself anywhere else in the world, and I knew my room-mate Adrian Timmis felt the same as we climbed painfully into our work jerseys and shorts and prepared for another day on the rack.

What I didn't know as we took the lift downstairs to breakfast was that our team manager, the man who'd dreamed up the madcap scheme of getting a British team into the Tour for the first time in 20 years, was at that moment squeezing his fat bulk into the team's Citroën turbo estate and was about to ride out of our lives. The man whom we'd come to rely on as our boss, paymaster and confidant was doing a runner.

I haven't seen Tony Capper from that day to this and my involvement with the team funded by Associated Nationwide Couriers and the bicycle shop chain Halfords, which was run by him, was to end in court on 28 June 1989, when I successfully sued ANC for wages that had been promised but had never arrived.

Within two months of the end of the 1987 Tour de France ANC Halfords had ceased to exist as a team, Capper had disappeared back to his tax haven in the Isle of Man and the team-van containing thousands of pounds worth of bikes and equipment had vanished, too.

So, if this book is about riding a bike successfully, about winning and losing, it's also about my fight to make a living in the most cut-throat, competitive sport in the world. It's about contracts and court cases as well as sprints and climbs. As my career has progressed, I've found a Capper behind every team in which I've been involved. Men for whom sponsorship and cash mean more than human beings. Men who accuse cyclists of being mercenaries just because they want a decent wage for the few short years they are involved in the roughest game of all.

In spite of everything, I can't say I dislike Tony Capper. I'm not going to dedicate this book to him but if he knocked on my front door now, I'd be civil, and I have to admit I wouldn't be where I am now – one of the top roadman sprinters in European cycle racing – without him. If Capper had never come into cycling I'd still be with an English team, earning bread and butter wages instead of the high rewards I've come to expect on the Continent.

British teams like Raleigh-Banana ride abroad now, but they have Capper to thank, too. He was the catalyst, he was the man who started it all off. Apart from my family, I have to admit that this rogue from Stoke-on-Trent has been the biggest influence in my career. Mine and many other people's.

But as Capper drove down the road out of La Plagne that day and left us to our fates, the good life seemed a long way away. That day I was at the top of a hill, but below was a valley and I was about to drop into it.

2. Sheffield Steel

Sheffield has hills – maybe not as high or as steep as the ones surrounding La Plagne, but as a training area for an aspiring cyclist they are almost perfect. To the west there are the winding passes and moors of the High Peak, while south are the rolling dales of Derbyshire. As a two-wheeled proving ground it is hard to beat.

It's no surprise to me now that of the 50 or so pro cyclists in the country a quarter of them live in or around Sheffield and South Yorkshire. It has become a real base, a hotbed of the sport. The city also contains my roots. Even now, although I've spent half my life away, I start feeling depressed when I haven't been home for a while. A lot of the time I might be in some foreign country, on the bike, and it's raining and the rest of the bunch are giving me a real hammering and the hotel that night is a half-star dump and all I am going to do is eat, wash, shave my legs, get a massage, sleep, then get back on the bike again: that's when I miss home. The 'glamorous' life of a pro cyclist is often more like being in prison and you suffer day after day to earn money for the time you can climb out of the saddle and start enjoying a normal life.

My early days could not have been more normal. My father

Jack was a keen touring cyclist, so in many ways the sport was inbred, but it was thanks to my mum Pat and my sisters Rowena and Hilary that I started. Rowena and Hilary had their own bike and by the time I was five, mum had taught me to ride it. She used to walk round the garden in Walkley, holding me on to it, but it wasn't long before I was off up the road – she wouldn't see me for a couple of hours after that.

I don't really know why, but I seemed to be pestering for a bike for a long time. Maybe money was tight or maybe, wisely, they didn't want me out on the roads at that age. But, on my eleventh birthday, I finally got the machine. All my spending money went on my little bike, buying new bits for it, building it up, and I was on it all the time. With a few friends I'd cycle out to Bradfield, about 5½ miles there and 5½ miles back – it would take us all day! We'd stop four or five times on the way there and wait for the stragglers and I'd say: 'What are we stopping for, let's get going.' I was always at the front even then, up there with guys five or ten years older than me. They'd go ahead but I'd chase and catch them up.

As I got older, one by one my friends lost interest and by the time I was 15 there wasn't anyone else riding a bike apart from me. I'd be going out to York and places like that on my own, about 110 miles there and back. With dad's prompting I joined the Cyclists Touring Club from Sheffield and went on a few slow rides with them, but it all seemed so sedate. Until that day in July 1976, when I saw my first road race.

I'd seen the race advertised in the city centre of Sheffield and I was just open-mouthed at the glamour of it. The colour, the whooshing of the tyres and the chrome flashing – I wanted to get into it. They were kids of my own age and I thought I'd love to be doing that, but how? They all had bikes worth hundreds of pounds compared with my £50 effort. I'd lavished all sorts of care and attention on my machine – even at that age I'd learned to do all the mechanics and could build a bike – but it wasn't a racing bike.

5

I knew, through dad, that the way into it was to join a proper club but I'd hesitated for ages. I was shy and I suppose I thought they'd laugh at me and my bike, but eventually I plucked up the courage and went on one of Rutland Cycling Club's Thursday night training sessions, just down the road from where we lived in Prescott Road. It seems funny now but I was so shy I didn't even like to wear shorts and just turned up in jeans and trouser clips.

There were about half a dozen riders there, all with flash bikes and I was out with them for about two hours keeping up with them until the last few miles when I was trailing and getting a few pushes. But by my second session I knew what to expect and I was prepared to force it a bit. I didn't need pushing again.

At the age of 15 fitness is not something you consider. If you want to do it then you just push yourself and don't think about it. It's only when you dig deep into it that you begin to find that cycle racing is 95 per cent fitness – and another 95 per cent dedication. There are some things you don't have control of, like the way you're built. My racing weight now is around 11 stones ten pounds, so I was never going to be a top climber. One kid in a hundred who rides a bike may have the natural ability to do well, but on top of that you need the application and self-denial. If you've got all those things and you really want to make it, then you can. But superkids like that are few and far between. That's why out of the 200 riders who start the Tour de France each year there are only five or six good enough to win it.

When I joined Rutland I was just thrilled by everything about cycling. It was something I wanted to do, so I did it, even though it hurt at times. I got myself some proper clothing and began to feel more the part. Within a month I'd ridden my first ten-mile time trial from Hathersage out to Castleton and back again. I clocked 25 minutes 49 seconds – you always remember your first one – and people around at the time said it was a good ride for a first time trial.

While I fitted in well with the club, at school I was what you might call a disruptive influence. I did well in my exams but then I'd just get fed up and I was with a gang of friends who weren't that bothered either. I suppose we dragged each other down a bit, but I don't really regret it now. If I'd left school better qualified I might have gone into a different kind of career and would not have got to where I am now in cycling. By the time I retire and start looking for alternative employment, when I'm 35 or so, I'm sure a few handfuls of exam papers or qualifications won't make any difference!

At school I was already dedicated to cycling and I just wasn't listening – it was a gradual downhill slide! On the bike I had one aim in life – I wanted to know what it would be like to win a race with my arms up in the air as I'd seen in so many photographs. By 1977 dad and I had built my own bike and I had started to win handicap prizes in time trials but looking back now I'm amazed at how green I was.

My first race was at RAF Swinderby, near Lincoln, just laps around an airfield. I started off in the wrong age group. On one lap a bell sounded and I wondered why the other contestants were accelerating. I didn't even know that a bell signified the last lap; and when we crossed the line I wondered why they were all slowing down! Why were they all turning round? I got disqualified for being in the wrong group, but once I'd sorted myself out into the right age group – and learned when the last lap was – I quickly started getting results.

I won the junior division in the North Midland Regional Championship and at a road race in Lancaster actually crossed the line first. I remember feeling disappointed that the crowd wasn't very big. It didn't seem like a proper race. But the event after that was the National Championships at Blenheim Palace and all the divisional champions from all over the country were there. Some of them were wearing champions' jerseys while I had my club jersey on. In those days the North Midlands didn't run to a champion's jersey. I finished second, beaten by a rider from London. The only riders still going that I remember from that occasion are John Wainwright from Sheffield and Mike Doyle. The three of us were the 'Class of '77' if you like and we rode all the races right through.

When I was 18, my name was in the local papers and people were talking about a golden future and all that. All I thought of was the next race and the points I needed for a First Category licence. After turning senior at 18 I rode five races in nine days and within 13 days of my birthday I had the 30 points necessary.

Selection for the National Junior squad followed quickly and in June 1979 I had my first trip abroad with John Wainwright and Dave Thompson from Thornaby. It was a three-day event in Frankfurt and I was placed fourth in a stage and eighth overall. It was hot and I wasn't prepared for it. But it was something different, a vast new experience that I wanted more of.

Just after I'd turned senior, I rode the Star Sprint in Sheffield, a one-lapper sponsored by the Sheffield Star with four heats and four riders in the final. I finished up in the final with Urs Freüler, who was the top amateur sprinter then, a real big hitter. There was another guy from the Swiss national team, and Paul Swinnerton who was a British sprint champion. I beat them all. Since then I've seen Freüler all over Europe after he turned pro with Panasonic. He's won stages of the Tour of Italy, and beating him and Swinnerton in Sheffield that day caused a bit of a stir.

At the time I saw myself simply as a road racer but then I was selected for the World Championships – in the pursuit. The training week was at Newcastle-under-Lyme and at the end of it the final selection for the trip to Buenos Aires was to be made. We had a ride-off against the Great Britain senior team, and we beat them, a scratch team of juniors. That was when they told me: 'Hey. you're a good pursuiter, we can do something with you'. So I finished up on the plane to Argentina to ride the road race and the team pursuit.

The pursuit team comprised Tony Mayer, Gary Sadler and Steve Denton. Tony Mayer is married to Frances Swinnerton whose sister is married to the well-known Irish professional Martin Earley – quite a cycling family. Steve Denton was a typical 'Barnsley-ite', really broad and so strong and talented. But he couldn't take the authority and discipline from the people in charge. He got suspended for something like double-entering for six months and got so choked off he just didn't start again, Last time I heard he'd taken up body-building. Gary Sadler later turned professional, too, and was riding up to about two or three years ago. He was a really good junior. Also out there were Darryl Webster, later to become my team-mate at Teka, and Mike Doyle.

At the age of 18, with a place in the Junior World Championships, my career seemed nicely on course, but within a week I was in hospital encased head-to-foot in plaster . . .

The team pursuit had come first with the road race scheduled for the following Saturday. We had been well on our way to winning the quarter-finals when the next thing I knew I was waking up in hospital with nurses and doctors trying to get my clothes off me. What had happened was that a medic had walked on to the track to treat another injured rider. I was third in line and the first rider managed to avoid him, the second skimmed him, while I stacked straight into him. I fractured a vertebra and displaced two others and I came round on my hospital bed in total confusion. I couldn't remember anything that had happened until ten or 15 minutes before the race. All I could think was, 'Let me get up, there's another round yet.' If Tony Mayer and I had managed to stay on we'd have won the round anyway, so we were *that* far off a medal, but he was in hospital with me and we had no team left. The road race was out, too. A certain Greg Lemond took that by default after the first man home was disqualified.

For a couple of years after that I used to have backache if I was standing up for any length of time which diminished gradually over the years and is now gone completely – but that was far and away the worst crash I've had.

When I was out in Argentina I was already short-listed for the Moscow Olympics and my horizons were gradually widening. I was working in Tony Butterworth's bike shop in Sheffield when the phone rang. It was Harry Hall who has a shop in Manchester. Harry was friends with a guy called Derek Harrison, an ex-pro living in Troyes. The club he'd ridden for out there, UV Aube, had asked him if he knew any English riders who fancied a spell in France. I thought it sounded like a good idea and persuaded a mate called Nigel Gilbert, who was also in the junior squad, to come out with me. So in February 1980 I was packing my bags to live away from home for the first time.

All the time I had to keep in touch with Willie Moore who was coach for the Olympic team and a lot of the time I was hopping back and forth across the Channel. I got on well with Willie. As an ex-rider he had my respect. He'd won a silver medal in the World Championships in San Sebastian, Spain, when it should have been the gold. One of the West Germans punctured and of course the British management, being true sportsmen, declined the gold and settled for silver. Willie, as a team manager, wanted discipline and respect and received more of these than most team managers I've been with. He wasn't like some who say go out and do whatever you want. He would give definite commands, like do two hours or 70 miles, do so much in such and such a gear or do one hour behind a motor bike.

You need that sort of discipline in a team event like the pursuit. You can't have four guys, who are competing as a team, just going off and doing their own thing. Track racing has some real pressure. You might turn up for a race at 4 p.m. and find there are other events on. The race might get moved forwards or back and all the time you are on edge. You might go and have a warm-up and get yourself ready – every rider has his own little ritual – and then discover your event has been postponed. The strain is tremendous. In a team pursuit if you make a mistake, a little technical mistake, you are letting three other blokes down as well as yourself. It's incredibly exhausting, mentally and physically.

So while I was out in Troyes I had to keep up with the training sessions back at the Leicester track. I won a couple of races out in France and Troyes gradually became my second home. It was hard at 18 to adjust to such a different lifestyle. But life was relaxed and three or four times a week Nigel and I would get invited to eat with families of other riders. That made it easier than having to cook for ourselves all the time. The first people I met over there were the president of the club and his wife, Jean and Marie-Francoise Legourvenec, and they used to look after us like their own children, washing for us and inviting us round to eat and drink and generally being very kind. There was no pressure, we just rode the races and enjoyed it – breaking even on the prize money so it didn't cost anything.

I was making a living from cycling already.

When Willie Moore announced the team for the Moscow Olympics it read: Malcolm Elliott, Tony Doyle, Sean Yates and Glen Mitchell. Glen later turned pro with the Percy Bilton team before he packed in cycling to take over his dad's taxi business, but the careers of the other three have remained intertwined ever since.

Sean was always a big lad but with something of the 'little

boy lost' about him. Tony used to rag him something awful, not in a nasty way, but Sean was an easy target and that used to spur Tony on. Tony was always the one who was thinking up practical jokes and Sean was usually the butt of them. I remember one occasion in Moscow. There was a lift going up to the eleventh floor in the hotel where the cyclists were quartered. On the way up we grabbed Sean, took all his clothes off, got him out of the lift at the top, then stuffed all his clothes in the lift on its way down. Sean was left starkers in the corridor. I don't think we'd get away with that now!

People who don't know any better have built up an image of Sean and Tony as bitter rivals who hate each other's guts, but it was others who created that rivalry. It was the individual pursuit in Moscow where it all started. It should have been decided long before who was going to ride that race, but for some daft reason it was decided to have a ride-off in Moscow, like a training run on the track one day. Tony won it – and Sean was still selected. Tony was the national champion, so I can't see on what basis they picked Sean, and putting riders under that sort of pressure just isn't fair. Despite all this, we managed to finish fifth in the team pursuit and set a world record which lasted all of 57 minutes.

Competing at the Olympics is supposed to be the ultimate in an athlete's career but Moscow could have been any town in the world for all we saw of it. You get on the bus to the venue, then back into the bus to the village – all you see is a bit of road on the way. Sometimes we'd get the bus into the city for a wander round, but they wouldn't accept roubles in the shops – only Western currency. There were no young people on the streets, they'd apparently been shipped off to Siberia or somewhere for the summer so they wouldn't be tainted with decadent Western ideas. As for the other athletes . . . well, cyclists are notorious for having little sporting interest outside cycling but the truth is we never saw any of them anyway. They'd be down at the stadium . . . we'd be out on the road.

I returned to France late in 1980, determined to put the track behind me. I thought I'd get myself a bit more established abroad, get a bit more experience on the road and learn the language, the lifestyle. There were other good riders around the Troyes area. Robert Millar, who I was later to join at Fagor, had turned pro that year and was living down there. Stephen Roche was an amateur with ACBB. Like me I think they knew that the professional scene back home was dormant and that to make any sort of impact you had to live and ride abroad.

My future in cycling was really decided when I won two golds in the 1982 Commonwealth Games in Brisbane, Australia, although when I went out to prepare I definitely wasn't in the best shape. All my sharpening up was done in the week before the 100 kilometres. I was the baby of the team at 21. Steve Lawrence, an ex-national champion, was 26 and he was the next youngest behind Bob Downs and Joe Waugh. Bob's the only one still going apart from me. Joe had been second in the Milk Race in 1976 to Bill Nickson and was a fantastic climber. Nowadays he builds frames up in the North-East.

The team time trial was up and down a 25-kilometre stretch of the Bruce Highway and the Aussies were favourites on their home ground. The time of two hours, nine minutes and 33 seconds looked unbeatable but in the last 25 kilo-metres we started to make some time up, clawing back 25 seconds, and with two kilometres to go I knew we were in with a chance. With 400 metres left the race commentator began the countdown for what he was convinced was an Australian victory. I went to the front and rode as hard as I could. I gave it everything until there was literally nothing left, pulled aside, sat up and the other three raced through to the line. We made it by six seconds.

Steve rode straight into the arms of his wife Suzanne while the rest of us embraced each other. The Aussies had a hard luck story about one of their guys puncturing but Joe had had chain trouble too and was forced to change his bike. So the excuses ironed each other out. Apparently the Aussie press were a bit upset, too, when Eileen Gray, the English national cycling president, presented the medals and gave all the Brits a kiss and a hug . . . and just a handshake for the runners-up!

I had a week between that race and the 184-kilometre road race and I got in some good miles with people like Jeff Williams, Mark Bell and Gary Sadler. Only four competed in the road race: Steve, myself, Mark and Jeff. The Aussies were pretty good at shouting about who were their favourites and most of them had their money on Remo Sansonetti. Canada's Steve Bauer, a couple of days before, had come second or third on the track and he was also well-fancied. For myself, I felt less pressure. The thought was I'd already won one gold so if I didn't do any more it was not the end of the world.

The race itself was a whittling down process. At one time a Welsh guy, Russell Harrington, got a couple of minutes, but with one lap to go we pulled him back and it came down to five of us . . . me, Steve Lawrence, Steve Bauer, Roger Sumich and Harrington. I still have the video of the finish – the whole race was covered live – and the commentators hardly mentioned me. One of them was Garry Sutton, Shane's brother, and I still have a dig at him about it whenever I see him. It was 'Bauer this or Sumich that' until near the finish when you can suddenly hear him saying 'Oh yes, we have the Englishman'!

It was a fairly orthodox sort of sprint. Nobody tried to attack on the run-in and I stayed down near the back. To Bauer and Sumich I was an unknown and I got the right wheels and went over Bauer fairly easy for my second gold. Since then, of course, Bauer's done quite nicely for himself. For me, too, this was the start of something big.

3. Top Of The Milk

With a record 17 stage wins over five years and an overall victory, I suppose the race most of the British public associate me with is the Milk Race. At over 1,000 miles and taking in most of the country, it's the nearest we have to one of the major Continental Tours – and it's the domestic race the home-based professionals would most like to win.

In 1983, I took six stages to go with the two I'd taken earlier in the year in the Sealink International. It was one of those years. I know I've won stages and races since then but I've never really experienced anything like that again. I think it was because I wasn't putting pressure on myself. I'd just go out and take each day and each stage as it came. I couldn't go wrong, getting on the right wheels all the time and knowing I had the power to go round anyone. I'd put the bike on the 12 sprocket, even uphill, and go round the other contestants, then throw my arms up in the air with ten yards to go. It was a fantastic feeling.

I was still officially an amateur riding for Great Briatin, but really I hadn't worked since 1980. There had been a tentative offer from Falcon to turn pro. But I was getting enough to see me by from sponsored amateur clubs like Manchester Wheelers and I didn't really know at that time what I was worth.

In the 1983 Milk Race, I took the prologue from Sean Yates and Tony Doyle – both pros by then – followed with wins at Ipswich, Burntwood, Liverpool, Hull and Middlesbrough, but later missed three vital breaks and had to settle for third place, although I was under no real illusions about winning . . . I was beaten by two men who were stronger and that was that.

There's a good atmosphere about the Milk Race, good organisation and good hotels and you get quite a lot of acclaim. I vowed there and then I would win it one day. It became one of my dreams.

It was at the end of 1983 that George Shaw approached me with a firm offer to turn pro with a new team he was setting up with Raleigh. I accepted. The previous year they had just had a single sponsored rider, John Wainwright. Now there were six of us, with me as team leader at £6,000 a year which wasn't bad to start with – there weren't many riders getting that much. As for the team set-up, I didn't care for it. We used to moan and gripe all the time about George and the bikes and the organisation and everything. George is my manager now and things are different but in those days all we seemed to do was give him stick behind his back.

We had a team car and John Wainwright, Nigel Bloor and myself used to travel to races in it. The trouble was that it was permanently stationed in George's drive and we always had to go through the ritual of going to George's house, picking it up and returning it after the race, even though George had two cars of his own. The car used to do about ten miles to the gallon and had a public address speaker on the roof-rack. We used to drive along and if we saw a dog in the road we'd bark at it through the tannoy. We'd play classical music at full blast going down the street.

I suppose it was behaviour like this that gave me a reputation as a bit of a wild man, but then I've never accepted the view that you have to live like a monk to be a professional cyclist. Before long I'd been lumbered with the 'playboy' tag, mainly because I wasn't as dedicated as someone like Sean Kelly. I liked my nights out and my beer, and still do. In the past I've done it to excess and for long spells at a time. But then I've perhaps had plenty to drink the night before a race and still gone well, so I don't think it has done much harm. I want to live a little, like a normal person, from time to time. I need my binges. I know some riders feel they have to be completely dedicated – no women, no drink, early nights and so forth – but for me it would have an adverse effect. In many ways I don't think the playboy image has damaged my career. It shows I have some personality. I've always liked nice cars and having a Porsche Carrera with a personalised number plate is all part of it. If you are a sportsman and carry on like a playboy and still deliver the goods, there's nothing anyone can say, is there?

I performed well enough in my first few pro races. I won the Sealink in April 1984 and got a number of placings in others. The big step from amateur to pro seemed easy enough and after riding with pros in the past, in competitions like the Milk Race and the Sealink, I certainly wasn't getting shot to pieces.

The 1984 Milk Race was dominated by the Russians who produced a formidable team performance and some strong individuals. I won the 107-mile opening stage from Brighton to Swindon in a hurly-burly sprint where I got my first taste of the Red Brigade's strong-arm tactics. I had Kashirin on my left when Czougeda, his team-mate, came up on my right, leaning in and trying to hold me on to his wheel to set up the win for Zinoniev. I had literally to fight my way out and went from about 150 metres to catch Zinoniev and take the stage, with 60 others charging behind. Over the years we became used to the aggressive tactics of the Russians – this was just a foretaste. Two years later the 1984 crew looked like choirboys alongside a certain gentleman called Abdujaporov, the

17

'Terror of Tashkent', of whom there will be more later.

I stayed in yellow for three days in 1984 but then got bombed out on the fourth hilly stage from Malvern to Swansea when I began to realise that maybe I was a bit too big to be a climber. From then on it was a Soviet procession until we got to Darlington on 6 June, where I took my eighth Milk Race stage and a new record, although even that was overshadowed by controversy. Four days before, John Wainwright had been ridden off the road and out of the race by some of the Russians and just before the start of the York-Darlington stage the race referee, Peter Whelan, had given them an official warning. Maybe that's why when we came to the last corner, the four Russians in front, instead of closing off the inside as they normally would have done, swung wide and I squeezed through the gap to win.

They turned the screw after that, with four stage wins in the next five days broken only by Gary Thomson's surprise win in Halifax. Czougeda had taken the jersey in Llandudno on the fifth stage and he never lost it again. The final 84 miles were ridden at a dawdle – about 22 miles an hour – and Czougeda, who many thought would crack in the mountains, beat me by a length in the sprint, when once again I found myself squeezed in on the rails as the Russian went clear.

I was happy with my record stage win and the £2,000 for the Hot Spot sprint, but life with Raleigh was still far from perfect. I needn't have worried . . . coming slowly over the horizon was a 20-stone, chain-smoking, Coke-swilling 'knight in shining armour' called Tony Capper.

Capper had appeared on the scene in 1984 with Mick Morrison in tow. Micky, a likeable and humorous chatterbox from Stoke, was his sponsored rider and apparently Capper had taken him aside one day and said something like, 'Son, I can make you a star.'

By early 1985 Capper and his company ANC had five riders – Micky, Phil Thomas, Joey McLoughlin, Dudley Hayton and Simon Day, with Phil Griffiths as part-time manager. It was a new team and I was impressed by what appeared to be a really professional approach. At races you couldn't really miss Capper and not just because of his bulk. He used to roll up in his big green Jaguar with a handful of cigarettes in his hand. So much gossiping goes on in cycling circles, anyway, and you couldn't fail to know who he was, what he was saying and above all what he was paying.

He certainly upset the establishment. A lot of the sponsors took exception to a guy who'd been around for just a year and thought he knew it all. He would put forward lots of ideas for big changes. His attitude was: 'Whatever you've done in the past, it's wrong.' He definitely caused resentment in people who'd been in the sport for years. Capper was keen to get involved and in the beginning there was a lot of distrust. There was also an undercurrent of feeling that maybe this guy was a bit of a rogue.

By the middle of 1985 my two years with Raleigh were dragging to a painful conclusion. In the 1985 Milk Race virtually all five members were wiped out in a big stack-up at Coventry. Mark Walsham dislocated his shoulder and Phil Bayton was badly bruised down one side. John Wainwright, Steve Jones and I were scraped about a bit. I was lucky really, because when the crash happened I was near a gap in the railings and went through it while the others piled up on top of each other. By the standards of 1984 I had a bad season but I still won the National Pursuit Championship, came third in the Kellogg's series and won two stages in the Milk Race. Raleigh, however, were supposed to have doubled the budget and were expecting more of a return.

We'd lost a lot of races we should have won that year. Phil Bayton was going so strong that he was just tearing people apart. He'd take people away with him in little breaks. We wouldn't chase him and then he'd get beaten while behind I was winning the bunch sprint. It was so frustrating. Then one day George got a letter from the sponsors. It said basically that Malcolm was supposed to be the leader but wasn't coming up with the goods and why not let Phil or Mark have a go? This, of course, was exactly what we'd been doing and exactly why we kept getting beaten. The letter really incensed me and I kept it for a long time after. I later showed it to a couple of ANC lads and they were astonished I hadn't walked out. I didn't walk out, but my days with Raleigh were clearly numbered.

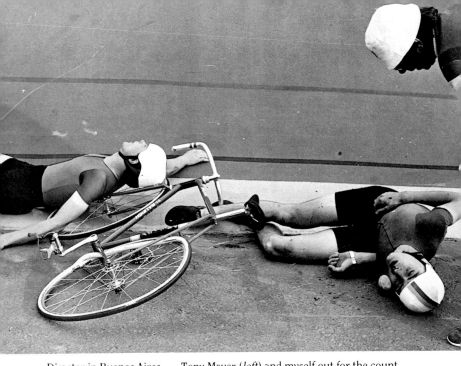

Disaster in Buenos Aires . . . Tony Mayer (*left*) and myself out for the count while team manager Jim Hendry looks on.

(*Left*) Putting on the pressure in the 1980 Grand Prix St Parres-aux-Tertres with future Tour de France stage winner Jerome Simon clinging on behind . . . (*J.A. Coulson*) . . . and (*right*) holding on to win with Simon and Régis Clere back down the road.

(*Above left*)　Celebrating my first win on French soil with Eric Gilbert, father of my old mate Nigel. (*J.A. Coulson*)

(*Above*)　Make them suffer . . . leading the 1980 Stannington Grand Prix with Steve Joughin and Les Fleetwood behind.

(*Left*)　Golden boy . . . on the podium at the 1982 Commonwealth Games in Brisbane.

(*Opposite, above*)　Lotta bottle . . . leading the charge into Liverpool's Sefton Park in the 1983 Milk Race.

. . . and (*below*) again at Middlesbrough in the same year. (*Graham Watson*)

(*Above*) Making a point to Tony Doyle at Ipswich in the 1983 Milk Race. (*Graham Watson*)

(*Left*) Wearing the Criterium Champion's jersey in the 1984 Kellogg's Series. (*Photosport International*)

(*Opposite, above*) The man with his eye on my wheel is eventual winner Oleg Czougeda with Ulrich Rottler (102) and Pete Longbottom (12) in the 1984 Milk Race. (*Mike Cowling*)

(*Below*) One jump ahead . . . the finish at Darlington in the 1984 Milk Race.

(*Right*) That's my boy . . . Capper introduces Joey McLoughlin to his fans. (*Graham Watson*)

(*Above*) In yellow in the 1986 Kellogg's Series in London (*Graham Watson*)

(*Left*) A hard lesson . . . after the 1987 Amstel Gold (*Graham Watson*)

(*Above*)   A crack with Kelly on the 1987 Tour de France. (*Graham Watson*)

(*Left*)   Winning by inches from Alexander Zinoviev at Hull in the 1987 Milk Race.

(*Below*)   Anything for a bet . . . Steve Jones and myself take the Russians by surprise . . . and they were expecting Pinta Girls!

(*Above*) Top of the Milk . . . in the final yellow jersey in the 1987 Milk Race. (*Paul Ibberson*)

. . . and (*right*) a kiss from mum after the 1987 victory. (*David Muscroft*)

4.   Capper's Boys

Capper's initial approach came through Phil Griffiths who as an amateur rider had been good enough to win a Milk Race prologue and still had lots of contacts among riders and in the trade – he still has. Phil was tied up with Capper's management company Action Sports and they were talking a lot of money for me to cut loose from Raleigh and sign up for them. I knew what I wanted, what figure I was after, and although he chipped me down a little it was still a lot more than in the past.

The deal was agreed in the back of his Jaguar in Nottingham amidst the polished woodwork and leather. Capper seemed very easy to do business with. A few thousand pounds didn't seem to matter with him, whereas in the past I'd had to haggle over the odd hundred. Lack of confidence certainly wasn't in Capper's make-up. He hadn't had the final say from ANC about a team for 1986 but he still signed a letter of intent with me to say he'd pay me whether he found a team or not. His attitude was: Sign now and I'll find the money later.

Capper was a strange figure to be involved in sport. He was so unhealthy, so overweight. He smoked almost non-stop and used to drink vast quantities of canned Coke and eat enormous amounts of cakes, sweets and pies. Driving along behind a race he probably put away more than all the riders together. I thought, this guy can't last much longer. He was 43 or 44 and looked about ten years older. I kept expecting to pick up a paper and read that he'd shuffled off. He was so anti-health himself but he was so into the sport, not just as a business – I think he revelled in the thought that we were his boys. I got to know him properly at the start of the 1986 season and he used to come out with this notion, this ambition, to get a team in the 1988 Tour de France. Our reaction was: Who's he trying to kid?

Not many of the riders were that bothered about it anyway. I used to think: What do we want to go into that for? None of us realised it at the time but this was the only way ahead. We'd started riding a few races abroad but a ride in the Tour seemed outlandish and we just humoured him. Capper was a trailblazer, I'll give him that. ANC were the first fully-fledged British team to compete abroad consistently.

In February 1986, we went over to Spain and rode the Ruta del Sol. It was a hard race then and still is, but we just went along and did it. It was good preparation, a chance to get out of the country in February, useful training. The Continental teams just ignored us, I think they looked on us as cannon fodder.

Micky Morrison was still with the team then and he used to keep us in stitches. We got there a few days before the start of the Ruta del Sol and we went out training, doing a few longish rides. They were hard roads round there and one day Micky got dropped – he was near the end of his career and was really only part-time. He arrived back about three quarters of an hour after us. We had all showered and changed and were sitting in the restaurant when Micky staggered in, hair all over the place, tongue on the floor and his eyes dangling on stalks. He shuffled across to us and gasped: 'What a stupid training ride, one in four for 50 miles. I'm not doing that again, I'm finished!'

The first stage ended in Gibraltar and Micky actually attacked and got off the front for three miles. They caught him on this bit of a track and he got shelled straight out the back, but what a character, just great for morale.

Even then the team organisation was good, given the fact that we were doing things that had been way beyond the scope of British teams previously. There were rough edges but there are rough edges with most teams, even those who've been in the game for years. The riders were a good mix. Apart from myself and Micky, there was Phil Thomas, Steve Jones, Graham Jones, Joey McLoughlin and Adrian Timmis. There was always a good crack, something I've missed abroad with Fagor and Teka. We would have plenty of laughs. One time Phil Thomas and I missed the start of a race at Alicante. We were directed the wrong way out of the hotel and couldn't find the start-line. We were like innocents abroad but we just didn't take it too seriously.

We were away most of February and March at things like the Ghent-Whevelgevm and Amstel Gold. Capper who lived on the Isle of Man as a tax exile would come and go, arguing with Phil Griffiths about this and that, full of an idea and having to be discouraged from doing it. The Tour of the Algarve seemed typical of his approach. Capper made a day of it, taking his wife along and Bill Bowers from ANC and his wife . . . the team went along, too, as a sort of afterthought! We did quite well there. Joey won two stages and I was third overall, although Joey and Adrian crashed with 20 miles to go on the last descent and finished up in hospital.

I found Capper a good motivator, although Joey found him hard work and too overpowering. Joey preferred the more subtle approach. I could take Capper with a pinch of salt but Joey needed tackling in a different way. As far as back-up went, mechanics and helpers and so on, Capper was a bit cavalier. He would invite people along and tell them: 'You pay for this or that and I'll see you right'. Of course he never did. Some got brassed off but we were the UK's most successful team so he could always find somebody else to tag along.

Joey's finest hour – and the team's – came in the 1986 Milk Race. After his crash in Portugal he had a big hole in his hip and wasn't sure that he'd even ride, but at Birmingham he was there for the start. All the team were going well from the off. I got second in the prologue to the Russian Sumnikov and warned for 'aggressive behaviour' in the first stage when Gary Sadler ripped all the spokes out of my front wheel on the run-in and there was a confrontation after the finish.

Aggressive behaviour? All I'd done was tackle him about it and he'd made an almighty lunge at me. I was really miffed about that.

After Sean Yates's second stage win I took the third on the split stage day at Harrogate after I'd clipped off with a Russian and a Belgian and they sat on me all the way. In the evening circuit race we had our first good look at the 'Terror of Tashkent'. Abdujaparov was and still is a very obnoxious rider. Very, very fast but just so unnecessarily aggressive in the sprints. If you wanted to get on a wheel and he didn't want you to, he'd just growl and lean on you. He upset everyone in the race. It got to the stage when there was talk of drawing lots and knocking him off his bike. And when it wasn't Abdujaparov, it was one of his mates.

On the fourth stage from Harrogate to Lincoln and with the next stage starting in Sheffield, I was determined to take the yellow jersey into my home city. But on the cobbled, one-in-six, last half mile to Castle Square, Zmievsky rode me right to the edge and I came to a virtual full stop as Abdujaparov escaped up the hill. Apart from that, ANC did everything right in that Milk Race.

By the start of stage seven, the Russian Petr Ugromov was leading, with Joey and I eight seconds adrift – the team competition was already in the bag for ANC. At the team meeting in Aberystwyth that night Joey seemed withdrawn into himself and I read the signs – he was building up for something. I thought if the race went on as it had done, with plenty of bunch sprints, I was going to win anyway. Either that or Joey would go away and win a stage by a good distance – and he was quite capable of that.

It was really hard country from Aberystwyth to Cardiff and, sure enough, Joey rode away on a fourth category climb and won the stage by about three minutes. The Russians, to our delight, just seemed to fold and we controlled the race behind easily. Of course, there was no way I was going to chase Joey down and I just sat back and enjoyed the sight of the Russians' panic. Their manager kept motoring up and down. One or two of them were consulting with each other and still nothing was happening. The gap went from two minutes to three minutes to four minutes and the Russian manager was going up to the front where Joey was to see that fair play was being done then back to scream at his riders while their heads were getting lower and lower.

When Joey crossed the line he was in tears and that was probably the high spot of the race. Even his eventual victory was something of an anti-climax after a performance like that, going away on his own and finishing with that kind of margin.

We were over the moon for him and the fact that for the first time the Milk Race looked like having a British winner. You look back now and think it's a good amateur race but then it was *the* biggest target.

In addition to Joey's victory, I finished second overall, took the points jersey, and ANC lifted the team prize, so Capper's dreams were beginning to look a little less far-fetched.

The Kellogg's City Centre Series began in Manchester that year. It's a long, pressurised race over five weeks, with points for each stage counting towards the overall championship.

Joey won the first stage in Manchester and I took the second in Dublin, although I didn't get any points for it because it rained and we rode a slippery road which meant cyclists were falling off all over the place. There were so many laps out that the organisers got totally baffled and decided that the result would stand but there would be no points for the Series: a bit of a cock-up.

By Cardiff I was in the yellow jersey and clinched it with third places in Birmingham and London but it cost me a lot. In the Kellogg's you have to hold your form for a long time and straight afterwards I took a dip. I started to come around in time to take third in the Welsh Championship and the Hotspots jersey in the Tour of Ireland before negotiating a new contract with Capper for what turned out to be my last year with ANC.

From the start of 1987 it was obvious this was going to be more of a Continental year. The team was the same minus Micky Morrison who'd stopped cycling, but Capper had also put together a Lycra Halfords team which was a canny way of sticking to the British rules of having no more than six in a team but having a dozen or so available for Continental racing. If we were riding at home, then nominally we were supposed to be competing against Lycra Halfords but actually we'd help each other. If an ANC rider got away, Lycra Halfords wouldn't chase, and vice versa. We'd split any prize money between the two teams.

As it so often happened, my early season form just didn't exist. We rode Het Volk in Holland, the Tour of Limburg and Paris-Nice which we'd managed to get into. Although I didn't realise it at the time, this was a good indication that we were going to get into the Tour de France as it's run by the same people. I did nothing in any of them. In Paris-Nice I finished second to last, with team-mate Paul Watson last, and I had a bad crash on the first stage into St Etienne and was pretty battered about.

The next day I lost a lot of time, so after that I was finishing in the back group every day. There were a lot of good guys in that group, guys like Planckaert and Bontempi so it wasn't just the no-hopers. Coming back from Paris-Nice I remember having the sorest legs ever. That was my biggest impression of one of cycling's great classics.

However, on 25 April I got my big chance to make an impression on a Continental classic. I also learnt a valuable lesson in home-town tactics which I've never forgotten.

The Amstel Gold is Holland's biggest race and being a classic is seen by most of the top team managers. I didn't know it at the time but also watching – on TV – were Stephen Roche and Patrick Valcke, his mechanic, who were later to play such a big role in my life.

For the first rolling 50 kilometres of the Amstel we just stayed together. It was a huge field and you tend to ride by yourself in these things. I didn't see any sign of the others for most of the race. On the Cruzeberg Hill I could see the field starting to splinter in front but I felt strong. I could see this or that good climber getting spat out and I wondered what was wrong with them. I was going up hard and still wasn't getting tired. There was a front group of about 20 on the run-in and I just sat back, doing as little as I could and responding on climbs and to one or two attacks. At each attack the bunch would get thinned down a bit more until on a short rise Steven Rooks attacked fiercely and before I knew it there were five of us left – Rooks, me, Bruno Cornillet, Joop Zootemelk and Teun Van Vliet. An Englishman, French-man and three Dutch. The five of us got together to keep the break going and I was having to work until, with 20 kilometres to go, the threat from behind had vanished. I remember Rooks going hard up a climb, Cornillet dropped off and I lost a couple of lengths. I was on the point of cracking when it levelled out again and I came round a corner to find the Dutch had stopped. They'd tried to get rid of me and failed and there were no more climbs on the run-in.

I tried to weigh up the opposition, three of the world's top riders, as we motored on, unaware that they had things sorted out by then. Zootemelk was about 40 at the time and I thought I'd beat him in a sprint. Rooks wasn't the rider then that he is now and in any case he had done a lot of the work. Which left Van Vliet, and I reckoned the other two had been paid off by him to sort me out and let him win. So I had my eyes on Teun and his wheel when all of a sudden Zootemelk accelerated slightly, got a gap, looked round then put his head down and went like stink. The other two more or less sat up and that was that. I could wave the win goodbye.

I knew that without them helping there was no way I was going to pull him back. Even if I could have, I'd have had nothing left for the sprint. In the end, with under a kilometre to go, Rooks attacked really hard up the outside and I was left to hold off Van Vliet for third. I'd been well and truly stitched up, but as Rooks and Van Vliet later admitted: 'What else could we do? We couldn't have an Englishman winning the Amstel Gold Race.' It sounds like conspiracy and I suppose it is but it's something I accept. I'd do the same thing on my home ground. My mistake was picking on Van Vliet as the danger.

Capper was slowly building up his squad for his assault on the Tour de France and ANC were becoming more and more international. We had a joint *directeur sportif* alongside Phil Griffiths called Ward Woutters, who apparently came as part of the deal for the cars we used abroad. We called him Muddy Woutters which seemed to suit him. He was quite a cold Belgian. You couldn't have a laugh with him and he had particular likes and dislikes – his main dislike being Paul Watson. Woutters didn't like the earring, the haircut or the independent attitude. At his best Paul was a zippy sort of rider and in a hard race he would stay with it but that year there was something up with him. He used to tell me: 'I'm not doing this for much longer. I'll give it a year or two then I'll be into something else. I've got other avenues like videos, graphic design.' They were his interests and he was trying to make a bit of money out of cycling to indulge them.

We also had two Frenchmen, Bernard Chesneau and Guy Gallopin. Chesneau wasn't a particularly talented rider but he was strong and proved useful in my winning Milk Race that year. Gallopin was President of the French Rider's Association and a very useful man to have around, highly respected and with lots of contacts abroad. He taught me a lot about other riders, their strong points and weak points and who to watch out for. Kvetoslav Palov was a Czech defector who was living in our house in Sheffield. He'd ridden the Tour of Lancashire as an amateur and Capper had signed him up. Steve Swart had appeared from New Zealand and he was brought in as a sort of reserve in case anyone took time out injured. And there was Shane Sutton.

Shane was the one who really stood out as a character, a typical pugnacious Aussie. There was one time when he got involved in a fight with Palov and Swart. It was a race abroad and Palov and Swart were sharing a room. Shane was next door. The lights were off and Shane's bed was right up against the wall. The partitions were really thin and we could hear everything through them. Palov was talking and sounding off about the team, saying things like, 'Malcolm, he could do this but look at him he's off out now with Paul on the town; Graham, he's past it, Shane he's knackered as well, he's not charging up . . .'

At that Shane got up, ran into the next room and set about Palov in the pitch dark. Swart had been sort of agreeing with Palov and Shane was trying to clock him too, but couldn't find him. Eventually Phil Griffiths came storming in and broke it up. After that Shane always kept Palov at arm's length. He'd say: 'Ah, that fellow Palov, how can you trust a bloke who'd run away and leave all his family behind?'

Graham Jones was a very experienced rider but I think he found that experience hard to pass on. He'd had a season back home with Ever Ready the previous year and he didn't quite come across as well as he should have done. I think he was still a bit dazed and numbed by all the years abroad as a pro. His whole career had been on the Continent and it must have been so confusing to find himself on the way back there – especially when we got on the Tour de France. That was the last thing he wanted.

Adrian Timmis at the time was very young, very quiet. He's come out of himself a lot since, although he still won't stick his neck out in company. Adrian is always conserving his energy, not getting drawn into anything, no arguments. He'd appear for a meal and then just go off on his own to sit and read. But he was capable of genuine brilliance. Two weeks before the Tour de France he won a stage in the Midi-Libre. There was a split on the run-in, someone jumped away and Adrian went across to beat him by a few seconds. It was a remarkable result. We were all stunned, thinking: 'Little Adrian's gone and done it. I wonder how he did it?'

We were remarkably laid back. I remember in the Midi-Libre, after the time trial, Paul Watson and I were riding back to the hotel along the sea front at Gruisson and saw all this windsurfing gear for hire. On a whim we just hopped off the bikes and had a go in our cycling gear. Ever since then, Paul always refers to that day as the Wind Surfing Stage.

In many ways the 1987 Milk Race was a foregone conclusion. Joey was out with his injured knee again and with the strongest team around I found myself favourite. As it turned out I wore yellow for the full fortnight. With Joey out, Palov came into the team, much to the disgust of Phil Thomas, Joey's brother-in-law and his logical replacement. At the last minute they formed a composite professional team and asked Phil to lead it but he was so brassed off he refused to wear the jersey and even covered up the Peugeot name on his bike and the ANC on his shorts. He refused to acknowledge that he was even part of the team – he wanted out and there was no way he was going to help us.

As it turned out, it was Phil who almost cost me the race before it started. In Newcastle I'd taken the prologue again from Mark Walsham by two seconds, and on the first leg proper ANC had had to chase down a break by Czech and French pros Philippe Casado and Philippe Louviet who got away for about 70 miles and were up four minutes at one time. Coming into Newton Aycliffe it was down to a bunch sprint and I was in the right place when Phil came through riding in the gutter. The normal thing to do in those circumstances is back off but he didn't and bounced off my handlebars to land in a heap. Sadly, he went on for another couple of days then went home.

I took that stage and the next two from Darlington to Hull and Hull to Lincoln and the press were talking about 'Unbeatable Elliott'. I knew different. No one wins three road stages without being lucky. I was on great form but in two bunch sprints and a sprint from a group of six there was so much that could have gone wrong – Phil found that out.

The stage I most wanted to win was into Sheffield, of course, and I lost out on that to the Russian Sumnikov, while local rival Mark Walsham beat me in the city-centre criterium the same night, much to his delight. That day I just couldn't do it. With both of us coming from Sheffield, and turning pro about the same time, I think Mark always thought he was riding in my shadow and when he has beaten me he's never resisted the opportunity to have a crow. After I joined Teka and won two stages in the Tour of Spain, my tyre rolled off in the sprint in a city-centre race in York and Walsham won it. Afterwards he said: 'Oh, it's OK winning stages in the Tour of Spain but it's a bit different round these narrow streets.' Mark's quite a good sprinter, but I think he's got a bit of a chip on his shoulder.

In the Milk Race the biggest danger to my ultimate victory didn't come from other riders, though. At Lincoln there had been a bit of a bust-up between the Lycra riders and the management. They wanted to know if they were going to get a bonus for my win. I had to phone up Capper and he started getting mad, saying, 'You're holding a gun to my head.'

Then the riders in the ANC team started playing up about bonuses and it got quite worrying. There I was in yellow, four days into the race, and everything was falling apart. They were all losing interest. People were getting quite upset about Phil Griffiths, too. Phil was always jumping down people's throats. They used to say: 'Oh, you're his favourite', but usually they were doing things I'd never do, like turning up to race with a dirty bike, or turning up late. Phil would get quite aggressive and it needed someone in the middle to try and calm things down. I found myself trying to do just that. Phil got annoyed, the riders were all brassed off and with eight days to go it looked as though I'd have no team to look after me.

Later on, after the Tour, Joey and Paul Watson produced a petition to oust Phil as manager. I told them to destroy it, but then Phil found out about it and there was more acrimony.

When the Milk Race reached the Peak District hills a lot of people thought I might crack, but I was back on familiar ground and on the sixth stage into Derby I put some of my local knowledge into good use. I knew there were some bollards in the road coming into the finishing straight and while everyone else went the long way round I went the short way and finished a good four lengths clear.

Sumnikov won in Malvern but really the Soviet threat in the race never materialised that year. They had plenty of chances to take control. On the stage into Birmingham they had five in a leading group, but ANC and Lycra just overpowered them. Alexander Zinovev was my nearest rival but on the Gloucester to Leicester leg I took a hot spot sprint at Southam. Then I beat him in the sprint for second place behind Pierre Le Bigaut to pocket another five seconds advantage, and by the time we arrived on Westminster Bridge on the last day the only thing that could have stopped me was a fall. ANC had ridden brilliantly tactically but I think I'd dominated the early part of the race so much that I'd left the field demoralised. My dream had come true. What I didn't know at the time was that the nightmare was about to begin.

5.   The Tour

Capper had performed the miracle – ANC Halfords were in the 1987 Tour de France. There was talk about stage wins for Elliott and a top 20 finish for someone like Adrian, but it didn't take long before the scales dropped from everyone's eyes.

The race started in Berlin and it was so hot, so humid, that we were wondering how we were going to get through to Paris before we'd even set out. On the night of the prologue, I just lay on the bed without any sheets, sweating away and unable to sleep, waiting for something to start that I knew was going to hurt.

I'd fancied my chances in the prologue and thought I could get into the top 15 or so. It was a long, curving road and I picked a line and tried to concentrate, keeping a smooth effort going, head down and seeing if I could get a bigger gear round. It seemed to be all over very quickly, except the last kilometre which went on for ever and ever. I was close to catching the rider in front, but some guys had gone 20 seconds faster. I knew how hard I'd tried and I attempted to find excuses: maybe I should have been in that gear, or maybe if I'd started faster . . . In the end I just had to admit that I wasn't good enough. The only solace I could find was looking at the results sheet and seeing the names of some of the superstars who'd finished behind me.

The stages in Berlin West were flat and fast and we just found ourselves sucked along from start to finish without having to give it much thought. We'd been shown up in the team time trial but then the low profile bikes had never turned up. We'd been promised them, along with carbon-fibre bikes for the mountain stages. I'd had a low profile bike early on in 1987 but it stayed as a frame hung up in Capper's garage. It never got used and as far as I know it was quietly disposed of for some poxy amount in the Isle of Man. In the team time trial every other team was on low profiles and disc wheels whereas we had five disc wheels between nine riders and rather than give the weaker riders an advantage we all went without. That sort of thing just makes you feel inferior from the start. This was the Tour de France, the pinnacle of the season and we couldn't even get a few extra disc wheels.

There were always reasons whenever you mentioned it. Capper would say: 'Lads, I tried but Campag let me down.' We were always asking for more kit and he'd say: 'I'm waiting for another delivery from Assos.'

There were other things that got on your nerves, too. Little things, but they all add up and on the Tour you can do without them. We had a Belgian *soigneur* called Roger who'd come into your room in the morning, swish your curtains open and bang on the bed to wake you up. That sort of thing rubs you up the wrong way.

Soigneurs like you to listen to them. Angus Fraser used to rub my legs and he was very good, but I'd have to listen to his problems. I'd say: 'How's it gone today. Angus?' And he'd start: 'My back was killing me in that car and the doctor's given me painkillers.' After a tough stage you wished you'd never asked. Sabino, the other *soigneur* would drive with one eye on the road and one on the pavement and was always pestering me to fix him up with an English girl when he came over for the Kellogg's Tour.

On the road, it had become a horror story. I remember the

stage from Karlsrühe to Stuttgart (we hadn't even reached France yet). So much of that stage was spent down in the gutter, clinging to the wheel up front and strung out in one single line. Who was going so hard in front, I don't know . . . I couldn't believe we were going so hard for so long. The hills were hellish – about eight third and fourth category climbs. The first one we went up, I remember starting near the front and within seconds being down in the last quarter of the bunch. There were gaps all over the place when we got to the top. Sutton and Chesneau were shot off the back and the thing that sticks in my memory is coming out of a town, looking up, and as far as I could see there was a long line of riders all out of their saddles and bikes weaving from side to side. You could see it coming down to you as each one sprinted to close on the wheel in front until it was your turn. I thought, 'any second now I'm going to blow', while all around me people were blowing and I'd have to go round them. We were supposed to function as a team but it was every man for himself. We were a bunch of individuals trying to survive.

We lost Chesneau on that stage and after Stuttgart I was in a personal crisis. I thought, if this continues there's no way I'll get to Paris, there's no way I'll even make the day after tomorrow. Sometimes I wished I would crack, just blow up completely, then I could have got out of it. But when you're in that line, suffering like hell, you just keep going, thinking it's going to ease up, it's going to get better.

At meals there wasn't much to talk about. No one would admit to what they were going through. Nothing else was happening in our lives except the Tour de France and most of that seemed to be happening somewhere else. We couldn't even have cared who won the stage. I'd look round the other riders and think nobody's feeling as bad as you, Malcolm, you're having the worst time. Only Gallopin looked bad. He was suffering and in low spirits. Perhaps what made it worse for him was that he knew what was coming each day. At least we were in the dark.

On the road from Strasbourg to Epinal we lost Graham Jones and Paul Watson. It was on the big climb of the Champ de Feu and everyone went past them near the bottom. At the time they looked OK and I thought they'd get back on the last group, but at the finish they were there. We got back to the cars and we could tell by their faces. I thought to myself, you lucky bastards, because at that moment I think I'd rather have been doing anything else anywhere in the world than riding the Tour de France. There was no help anywhere else, either.

Capper and Griffiths were quite understanding but it was as much of an eye-opener for them and they were at loggerheads with each other anyway. A lot of the time they weren't even speaking to one another. There were other English speakers in other teams but there was nothing much they could say to us. Kelly and Roche we knew quite well from riding the Kellogg's in Dublin and the Tour of Ireland but with Robert Millar it was as if he resented us being there. I got the impression that he was thinking, what do this shower want to come and get battered in the Tour de France for? It was only on the seventh stage and the run-in to Troyes that I actually started to enjoy a day. It was the nearest I'd got to going home and after the nightmare of the first week it was like waking up to familiar surroundings.

I was learning all the time, where to position myself and when to move up. I was pretty legless from the first week and was just getting sucked along by a nucleus of the world's top sprinters when we came round the last left-hand bend. The riders in front were making their final effort when all of a sudden there was this almighty whoosh! The huge figure of Guido Bontempi came past on my left, going about five miles an hour faster than anyone else. Kelly had just swung out to go round someone when Bontempi came charging through, clipping Kelly and bouncing him sideways. Bontempi never even slowed down. Quite impressive!

I'd finished tenth, well beaten, but just getting involved lifted my morale a bit. That and the thought that we were on to some flatter stages and the race was becoming a bit more established. But it was only a lull in the hostilities. The next crisis came in the time trial to Poitiers, 87 kilometres of sheer murder. In a long, flat time trial you're in the saddle most of the time and the pain in your backside is incredible. At the finish I tried to get off my bike but my legs went. I was too smashed to stay on but if I got off I wouldn't be able to stand up. Angus was trying to sort me out but I really thought I'd screwed the rest of the race up there and then.

Still the low profile bikes hadn't arrived and the carbon-fibres were waiting in the mechanics' van to be built up. In the end I never got one. What happened was that Capper had got hold of some daft hats with radios – about five hundred quids worth – off Jan Raas, the manager of the Dutch SuperConfex team. Naturally, being Capper, he never paid him for them. After Capper did his runner at La Plagne, Raas came looking for his money and Griffiths had to give him a brand new carbon-fibre bike in payment. That incident was typical of Capper. He was like a magpie. He'd see something and say: 'I want that.'

If I was in a state, Shane was worse. On the stage out of Poitiers, all the roads were melting. it was so hot. Shane finished the day 32 minutes down, having had long periods of hanging on to the car which cost Capper a bomb in fines. His reserves had gone and he was just riding on guts. Yet even though he was absolutely battered he would still make us laugh. He'd stagger in at the end of the day and he'd have a joke to tell about how he was hanging on to the car and some spectators had made some comment about it and he'd told them where to go in his best Aussie-French. He'd also rung home and found out that he hadn't been paid – nobody had – but then we just put it down to the Tour de France and the strain on the office organisation. At the time we never realised that we'd seen our last pay cheque. Capper had thrown us off the scent. At Strasbourg he'd sat me down and talked about 1988 and what he was going to pay me and what the team was going to look like. It was a sort of combination of him being very clever with his bluffing and also deceiving himself that it was all going to happen.

The closest I came to a stage win was at Bordeaux. The closest that year and the closest since, although I had a load of top ten finishes in 1988. On the way in I'd won four special primes and I felt so powerful. It was one of those days that come round only three or four times a year. You accelerate and feel so strong that you know there's no way you can be beaten. It was the first time in the race we'd had a circuit finish and I had a good look at the finish the first time we went through so I knew how to judge it and where to place myself. I had good legs that day, too. On the last corner, with 400 metres to go, Davis Phinney came past. I thought of going with him but then I decided he'd gone too early so I'd stay where I was. It strung out a bit round the corner. I was tucked in nicely, ready to make a great effort when there as a big crash in front. It's like a bad dream when that happens. You start seeing riders folding in front of you, hitting and bumping and falling over and you know there's going to be a crash and scraping of skin and you're flying right at them from behind. Looking back at the video now, I can see how wide I had to swing to get round. And that was it: Phinney first, Van Poppel second and me third. As I've pointed out, there is a lot of luck involved in sprinting.

That was a good day for crashes. After about 50 kilometres the jungle drums started beating that Kelly had gone. We heard he'd crashed virtually before he picked himself up. He came back to the bunch looking distressed. He has an anguished expression when he's trying but this was different. He'd lost heart, he looked more like a little kid, not like a hard man at all. But then it's a big thing if you've set your sights on winning the Tour and failed – it only comes round once a year. People are watching you and building you up to it and you feel as though you've let them down.

Shane packed in on the first day in the Pyrenees. He was disappointed but you could really see in his face he was missing his wife and kids – that was all he was talking about, going home to see them.

In the mountains, whether it's the Alps or Pyrenees, there's no pressure on me. I'm not saying I enjoy them but in many ways it's like a day off. There's not a lot to be gained for me whether I go 70 per cent or 90 per cent on a climb – I'm still not going to stay with the real climbers, so why waste more energy than I have to? On the climbs I would get five or six of the sprinters with me. It is the same group every day in the mountains. You might look up the road and see a little cluster in no man's land so you shout up at them 'grupetto!' Some of them might crack and think, there's a nice little group behind, I'll stick with them. What you're trying to do is to recruit as many members to your group as you can. Once the 'grupetto' is formed not many people get shot out the back unless they're in real trouble, but even then we're going so slow they can always catch up on the descent. 'The more the merrier' is the motto. It's called the laughing group, although there's precious little laughing goes on.

After three days in the Pyrenees I was still alive, if not actually kicking, and looking at the Tour map in Millau I began to think, yes, Malcolm, maybe you can get to Paris after all. I knew there were the High Alps to come, harder, higher than the Pyrenees but with better roads, not as bumpy or dangerous. I also figured out that the chances of flatter stages were few and far between – Avignon, Dijon and Paris. I thought winning in Paris was too wild a dream so I thought

I'd give it everything the next day into Avignon. If not it would have to be Dijon . . . not too far from Troyes and back on familiar territory again.

On the fast run-in to Avignon I got into about four moves. I was desperate to get into any move even though it may have been taking it out of me for the sprint. I wanted people to start seeing me, I wanted to be on TV for once. I was in the Tour but people could have been excused for not knowing it. After a lot of struggling I got into a break with Phil Anderson and the first thing to do when that happens is look around and see who's with you. The composition of the break didn't seem right and of course there was a rider from SuperConfex in lime green sitting on for Van Poppel. As ever, Raas hadn't missed the move. He had his guys drilled like a bunch of squaddies. Van Poppel took the stage and I couldn't help feeling jealous of him with all those work-horses slaving for him, although I could never see myself in that team. I've always found them a bit of a dour bunch, they never seem to have much of a laugh.

But then we weren't laughing much, either. At Avignon Capper's missus arrived with two of their kids and Capper decided they could sit with the riders for meals. That was the last thing we wanted, a couple of brats sitting around asking questions, making comments. They were tactless at the best of times but at the end of a hard stage and after two weeks of continuous racing – the hardest thing you'd done in your life – you just want to be on your own, with your own kind. We had to tell Capper: 'Tony, we don't want your kids around.' That upset him, but they left with Mrs Capper.

On the first day in the Alps Steve Swart was gone, leaving just four ANC survivors. In the last week it had become a matter of honour for everyone to finish. Having got that far we were close to being able to say: 'Yes, I finished the Tour de France', rather than 'Yes, rode it but I didn't finish it.' Swart was the one rider I thought would never pack in. He had a problem with his foot, but he just seemed so laid-back. His attitude seemed to be, it doesn't matter, it's only a race, it's only the Tour de France, we'll get through it. His morale seemed the best of anybody's.

Adrian was digging deep – not so much with the difficulty of the race, but with the duration of it. When you start a race as long and gruelling as the Tour de France you might as well be looking ahead to the end of the year if you contemplate finishing it. In the last week, when you try and think back to the start, it seems a lifetime ago. So much happens in those three weeks, every day is a whole story, 21 chapters in your life in as many days.

In the Alps, Alpe d'Huez was the hardest stage, but really all the stages roll into one. It's legendary but at the end of the day it's just another bloody hill you've got to get up, another day when nothing nice is going to happen to you. Some friends from Sheffield were there on the roadside, but there was no stopping for a chat. Nigel Gilbert was there and nearly got into a fight with a guy for giving me a push. I thought I'd get into trouble for it, but everyone gets a push. The Dutch are masters at it. There have been riders I've left at the bottom of the climb who I thought were minutes behind when they've come flying past me at the top without even turning the pedals – just getting one continuous push. As soon as one lets him go, another takes over and they just come hurtling past and out of sight. They aren't guys who are going to win a stage so it's no skin off my nose – if only I could get the same treatment!

The closer Paris got, the more my morale picked up. I started thinking, the scenery looks better, the food tastes better; the cloud, the big black cloud over me for two weeks was lifting.

At Dijon I had a good time trial but went wrong on the run-in when a gendarme sent me down the deviation for the team cars. I was doing nearly 40 miles an hour with a tailwind and I thought he was signalling at me but he was signalling to the car behind and I had to turn around and lost 20 seconds. So when I could have finished 14th or 15th I finished up 20th, but I didn't really mind. We were home and dry.

Everybody had been telling us how easy the last stage into Paris was, but someone must have changed the script because it was very hard. Fignon attacked virtually from the start and we spent about 20 miles on the rivet before they eased up. I remember gasping to Adrian: 'I thought this was supposed to be easy.'

When we got over the Pavés des Gardes, a brute of a dual carriageway that went way up, we could see right over Paris and that traditionally is when the ceasefire is lifted and the real racing begins. But I looked down and thought, I've made it. It was a terrific feeling, seeing the Eiffel Tower and looking round at everyone else and knowing that they're thinking the same thing. I've never known such a huge sense of achievement in just actually finishing a race.

When it was all over Guy and I sat on the team car bonnet for the lap of honour, wheeling our bikes alongside. We weren't going to ride one kilometre more. Up on the podium, Stephen Roche was climbing into his final yellow jersey. Although I didn't realise it at the time, my star was going to be hitched to his for some time in the future.

6. Wanted Man

After the Tour de France we had ten days before the Kellogg's
Tour of Britain, but as far as cycling went my head had gone
– I wanted to forget everything about it. I borrowed an ANC
car and drove with some friends to Biarritz. I became a beach
bum, riding for about an hour and a half a day, two or three
times a week and sunbathing the rest of the time. I started
having late nights and bingeing, doing all the wrong things,
but I just needed some release. Again I had to pay for it.

On the second stage of the Kellogg's, from Newcastle to
Manchester, Joey McLoughlin, who had hardly raced all year
and was raring to go, went away in the break. I was having
terrible problems with my guts. I was in such pain I was
hardly watching the race so when the break went there was
nothing I could do about it. I just had to pull in and drop my
pants by the roadside in an effort to get some relief.

By the time we reached Birmingham at the end of the
third stage, Joey was second, about five seconds behind the
jersey and we were riding for his win. At the Holiday Inn that
night two guys in suits turned up and introduced themselves.
They were acting on behalf of ANC. Mr Capper was no longer
involved with the team, they said, 'but don't worry, lads, ANC
will honour everyone's contract. Now just carry on with
exactly what you're doing like good little boys and everything

will be all right. Oh, and by the way, here's £350 each to tide you over.'

Most of the team were two months or more behind with their pay, so morale didn't exactly climb sky high. I was worried. It meant everything Capper had talked to me about had now gone by the board. Halfords were still supposed to be keen to run a team on their own, but I found them hard to pin down. By this time we all knew Joey and Adrian were going to Peugeot and we needed to find replacements for them and quick. I found myself as the go-between and Halfords kept telling me: 'We'll know something definite next week.' But next week never came.

In the meantime, we had to fulfil our professional obligations and take Joey to his Kellogg's victory. Then we were off on the Nissan Tour of Ireland. In cycling you can't just down tools – you must stay in the public eye. Basically, it's no different from any other sport . . . as long as you're winning or just performing well, you're in demand and can rely on regular pay days. But after the news about Capper and ANC I couldn't see many pay days ahead.

As we flew to Ireland for the start of the Nissan, my morale was about as low as it has ever been. I was out of shape and back in the old habit of late nights to break up the boredom. I knew deep down that I had to snap out of it and try and sell myself, although at the time I felt I had precious little to sell.

Two nights before the Nissan began I'd been out until five in the morning and when the racing started I paid for it. The first 100 miles from Dublin south to Waterford were purgatory. My legs felt like wood. Suddenly, however, on the run-in I began to feel better and in the last kilometre I felt very good indeed. But no-one was more surprised than me when I actually won the sprint from Marnix Lameire and Sean Kelly. At the finish I saw Joey coming in and he shook his head in amazement – he couldn't believe it either. It was inexplicable. I'd done nothing in the way of training since the Kellogg's, didn't know what was going to happen next year and didn't even have an incentive to carry on. I'd abused my body and yet here I was winning a major tour stage. But that's cycling. One minute you're down and the next minute you're in yellow. Suddenly I found myself in demand. Word got round that I was looking for a team. Z-Peugeot, Hitachi and Système-U all made approaches for the 1988 season. So did Stephen Roche, the world champion, and his new Fagor team. Then I won again three days later into Limerick, and in the final parade stage into Dublin my price went up a bit more. My bargaining power was going up almost daily.

If all this sounds mercenary, fair enough. But a cycling career is short and it's not a charitable thing. It's every man for himself and you have to do your own deals. My philosophy is to do what you can for yourself and don't worry about the other guy. If somebody whom I thought inferior as a cyclist was making more money, then I'd worry. But the thought that Roche gets something like £350,000 a year doesn't upset me – he's worth it. A lot of people think we're well paid and it's a cushy life but they forget that by the end of the year I'll have competed in 130 races and on top of that there's all the training, and I still have to be more disciplined than the average man in the street. Compared with golfers or tennis players we're paupers.

In cycling you don't get much free time on your own so you have to look after business deals whenever the opportunity arises. In the Nissan most of the bargaining was taking place on the road – during the race. One minute Cyrille Guimard, the *directeur sportif* of Système-U would pull up alongside in the team car for a chat, then I'd go back for a wheel and Roger Legeay of Z-Peugeot would tackle me. Then Stephen himself would roll up alongside and we'd talk some more.

After those stage wins it would be tempting to say that I

felt a lifting of morale, but really I didn't have any morale to be lifted. What I didn't know at the time was that Roche already had me pencilled in as the Fagor sprinter for 1988 and what Roche wants he usually gets. He'd spoken to Patrick Valcke, his nominated *directeur sportif* and I think Patrick looked on me as a sort of challenge. Even today he still addresses me as 'Playboy' in a sort of semi-joking way. Roche and Valcke were talking the same money as Guimard and the rest but the difference was that it was the leader of the team who wanted me, not the manager or the sponsor, and there were English speakers in the team already – Sean Yates and Bob Millar.

Système-U could have turned out very good or a complete disaster. At the time they had no foreign riders and Guimard is said to be difficult to get on with. He has his favourites and if you're not one of them it's tough. I was reluctant to go to Peugeot, as it meant going back to Joey and Adrian and I'd have been in the same sort of position as in the past. I might have got roped into situations where I was working for Joey again like in the 1986 Milk Race and I wanted to avoid that. Fagor, however, seemed a more cosmopolitan set-up.

When you're thousands of miles away from home for most of the year, that's important. It's good to see a face from home and hear a familiar voice. I speak French but when you're over in France for so long it's hard to keep adjusting: one minute you're speaking French and the next minute you're speaking English again. I notice now when I come home after just two weeks abroad, that it's a bit uncomfortable to start speaking in my native tongue again. You literally go from one environment to the next within hours and every few days you're adjusting, like: Is it *une petite bière* . . . or a pint today?

After the Nissan ended in Dublin I passed Roche in the corridor of the hotel in O'Connell Street where we'd changed. He was still in his racing kit and we were dashing off to catch the plane. He said: 'Don't sign for anybody else. You'll come and ride with me at Fagor.' That did it.

I don't have many heroes in my life – apart from David Bowie – but in cycling I guess Stephen Roche is the nearest. I'd first heard the name when I went over as an amateur to France in 1980 but we didn't get on talking terms until the Kellogg's tour of 1984 when after the final reception I found myself on a night out with him and a few others. I was glad to see he liked a few beers and didn't believe in going to bed at nine o'clock every night. I suppose I felt some justification for my own excesses. The thing that impressed me most, though, was his professional veneer – he's always polite and civil to the fans and the press. Not that he can't be a hard man when he needs to be.

I got closer to Roche on the ANC Tour de France when I saw him occasionally at the start of stages, but for most of that race he might have been on a different planet. That year he was absolutely the best cyclist.

So, when Roche began to stick his neck out for me I was flattered, and on 9 October 1987 I flew out to Lille, Fagor's French base, to sign a one-year contract with a two-year option. I went off to winter on the Sun Tour in Australia, happy at last and looking forward to the 1988 season for the first time in months.

Fagor and Roche had decided to announce their new line-up at a press conference in San Sebastian, Spain, on 3 January 1988 and I flew out from Britain ready to do my bit with the media. Within a couple of hours I was wishing that I was back with Capper and ANC.

7. Fagor Fiasco

Stephen Roche's biggest virtue — some say it's his biggest fault — is that he always stays loyal to anyone who's helped him in the past to the point of obstinacy. He tries to keep everyone happy and it can lead him into difficulties at times. That's why Patrick Valcke, who began as a humble mechanic and *soigneur* with Roche in his early days and then stayed with him through the thick and thin of the Tour of Italy when everyone, even his own team, were against him, gradually found himself promoted, until eventually part of Roche's contract with Fagor stipulated that Valcke would go along — as *directeur sportif*. Another guy who had stood by Roche was Phillipe Crepel who was going along as team manager, along with rider Eddy Schepers who had been at Roche's side virtually throughout their careers.

Unfortunately, by the time the riders got to San Sebastian in January for the photo call, Fagor, who are Spanish-backed but French-based, had suffered a dramatic change of heart and we walked right into the middle of a real old-fashioned Latin row. The first thing we read when we arrived at Orly Airport at 11 a.m. in the morning *en route* to Spain was a report in *L'Equipe* that Crepel was out and Valcke wouldn't be far behind. The team was breaking up before I'd even put on their jersey. Here we go again, I thought. It was the first indication that Fagor were going to be difficult people to deal with.

Roche was obviously deeply unhappy about the way things were going and when we arrived in San Sebastian at 11.30 that night, he called a 'union meeting' on the spot. Miguel Gomez, the commercial director of Fagor, turned up and there was a major shouting match.

'What the hell is going on,' Roche asked Gomez.

The Spaniard must have thought, with 15 riders and some personnel there, that we were trying to gang up on him and he became totally unreasonable. He was ranting and raving and we were getting nowhere, so Roche and Robert Millar took him quietly to one side in an effort to calm him down. Outside, the Spanish press and photographers sat impatiently, waiting to take pictures of the team that was supposed to take European cycling by storm.

At 1.15 a.m. the three re-appeared. They had got nowhere, but we were told that Augustin Mondragon, the Fagor chairman, was going to appear later that morning for a meeting. At nine o'clock we faithfully walked down to meet Mondragon and Gomez while the camera crews and pressmen shambled in and got ready again. Eventually Mondragon lost his patience and gave us an ultimatum: 'Crepel is out, take it or leave it.'

We got together for a ten-minute team meeting and went back to him: 'We'll leave it.'

One week later I was back on the same plane at the same time to San Sebastian. This time the photographers got their snaps of a Fagor line-up all smiles. Crepel and Valcke were staying on, at least for the time being, and Roche had agreed to a new three-year contract. The truth was that he had signed for a year but the lie Fagor issued was the price he had to pay to keep his friends on the payroll. Lesser riders in the team like Robert Forest and Jean-Claude Bagot who had stood up to Mondragon hardly got a ride in Fagor colours again. Such are the politics of cycling sponsorship.

Still, the rest of us had to get on with the job and that job was riding a bike. Early season training was down on the coast at Denia and from the start the atmosphere was more businesslike than I'd ever been used to. With ANC there had been time for a few laughs, but this was subtly different. At the launch Roche had introduced me and told them: 'This is Elliott, he's going to do well for us this year', so the pressure was on right away.

I told them that it took three months of the racing season to get to my best and there was nothing I could do to change this, but it made no difference. They had committed us to the early season Belgian events and I was sweating about that. I could see two or three months ahead of clogging around Belgium in races where it rained all day and I would be bouncing up and down on cobblestones and then going back to a miserable cold hotel in my wet gear. The one thing that kept me optimistic was the thought of getting Roche back from injury and into the form he'd reached the year before.

Our first race was the Grand Prix d'Albacete about 120 miles from Denia and I finished quite pleased with a seventh place in the bunch sprint behind Mathieu Hermans, but the team-work didn't seem to be there. I didn't want any organised help before I'd settled into the racing but really throughout the season there were few times when the team gelled well.

Two days later we did a training race up at Morvedre near Barcelona where I rode 169 kilometres then took a short cut to the finish to avoid all the nasty climbs. The next day I was tenth in the Trophy Luis Puig, so I was getting results even though there were guys in the team riding better than me who were getting nothing.

The Tour of Sicily more or less put me off riding in Italy for life. On the first stage I got fourth to Bontempi – about the nearest I've ever been to him in a sprint that he's won – but the racing was crazy. In a normal race you may find ten possible hazards in a kilometre . . . in Sicily you had 50. There were holes in the road, kerbs that jut out into the middle of the road, enormous grates that run lengthways so that you ride your tyres into them, dustbins – big wheeled dustbins just pushed into the road, cars all over the place, dogs and kids running out, scooters flying across junctions in front of you without stopping, and crazy riders, the craziest.

There were so many hazards I just didn't bother sprinting. Bontempi is an Italian, but it was obvious he was thinking the same, something like: hang on, it's a bit too early in the season to wipe myself out. It just wasn't worth it. And all the time there was still no sign of our leader. Roche was off his bike with a longstanding knee injury. Maybe if he'd been there he would have been able to sort out a lot of the shortcomings, the things about Fagor that got us down.

Sean Yates is a quiet, laid-back type. He doesn't complain much. He keeps things to himself and doesn't rely on other people, but he'd seen how things had been with Fagor the previous year and told us some real horror stories. At some races he'd been afraid to get on the bike because he knew the mechanics had been dragging their heels. Perhaps they hadn't glued the tyres to the rims properly in which case he knew they stood a good chance of rolling off down some mountain hairpin. Pierre Bazzo, the team manager, apparently used to go out on the town at night and he'd take the mechanics with him, the guys whose competence and clear heads your life depended on.

Millar was the next strongest rider in the team after Roche and the logical choice to step into the captain's shoes, but he didn't want the responsibility. He didn't want people hanging on his every break. If he was capable of doing a good ride, then that was fine, but he didn't want it at the expense of the team. But the Fagor fat cats started putting the pressure on.

They'd increased the budget dramatically from the year before. They were paying Roche a small fortune and they wanted results.

By April there were rumblings about Valcke. Mondragon had summoned him to San Sebastian for a dressing-down and Valcke had refused to go. At the hotel in Lille he came into the room I shared with Sean and asked if he could use the phone to call up Mondragon. He spoke to Gomez, a real pain in the arse, and told him: 'I'm not flying down tomorrow because I know there's no point. I realise you've given me the sack but just let me say this . . .' Then he told Gomez something in French which, translated literally, means 'You will remember the voyage, you won't forget this.' He called the team secretary and gave him a mouthful of abuse, put the phone down and that was it. That was the end of Patrick.

I was devastated and morale in the team fell about 80 per cent. He was a good bloke and had his finger on the pulse. He cared for the riders and things had begun to improve. Fagor's official line for firing him was that he'd been flirting with other sponsors while he was still contracted to them but there's nothing wrong with that. All the team managers do it, they've got to. Otherwise, when they get to the end of a season and the current sponsor pulls out, they're left high and dry. The real reason for firing Valcke was that he wasn't a 'yes' man. He stood up for himself and for the riders if he didn't like something.

Fagor had had complete control in the past but when Roche come along, bringing Valcke and Crepel with him, they started calling all the shots and Fagor didn't like that. When the crunch came it turned out that Roche hadn't got a 'watertight' contract. Perhaps he'd fallen for the old verbal agreement. Gomez and Mondragon and the others at Fagor would always use the phrase: 'You don't need it in writing, you've got the Basque handshake on it.' The number of times I've heard that!

So one day Valcke was in charge and the next day we woke up to find Bazzo back as *directeur sportif.* Bazzo was the ultimate Fagor 'yes' man. When Valcke arrived he'd been in charge of the team but soon found himself moved sideways. Now he was back in charge. His first act was to call us down to a team meeting and discuss the next day's racing. He talked to us as if we were a bunch of juniors: 'You've got a hill at 30 kilometres, another at 50, a narrow part at 90 kilometres . . .'

I remember catching Bob Millar's eye across the room. We were both thinking the same thing: 'What a prat!' I was biting my tongue to stop myself laughing but it really wasn't funny – we had to go and ride the Tour of Spain and Tour de France with this man in charge. As a bloke I had nothing against Bazzo. It was just his general attitude that I didn't like: he seemed so careless and casual. He didn't inspire us, he made us feel as if he was just there for the ride.

In the meantime came the news we'd all dreaded. The doctors had been into Roche's left knee again. Four times they'd had to cut him. It was certain now we'd be riding Spain and France without him.

After the Tour de France, the Tour of Italy and the Vuelta – the Tour of Spain – are considered the next in importance. The Vuelta is 21 days without a rest day and there's some very big mountain stages. I'd heard bad reports: that it was a really hard race and that the Spanish teams would do their best to murder all the foreign opposition. It was supposed to be a difficult race for riders, with basic hotels, bad food, bad weather. You could get sick or injured in some primitive part of Spain and find the medical back-up was second-rate.

When I joined Fagor, Valcke's plan had been for me to ride some of the early season classics like the Amstel Gold and Four Days of Dunkerque which were better races for me. That was the plan, but once they got rid of Valcke they kicked it out. I had just ten days notice that I was going to Spain and the Vuelta. With 40 mountain passes to be crossed and five stages finishing on climbs, all in early May, I definitely was not looking forward to it.

The 1988 Tour of Spain began like an island-hopping expedition. The prologue and first stage were in Tenerife, then they flew us over to Gran Canaria for a team time trial before landing on the mainland for stage four from Alcala del Rio to Badajos. I got third there, then a second on stage six from Bejar to Valladolid. Hermans was going like a train, though, and I was soon down to fifth or sixth. I seemed to be going backwards. So was my morale. I began to think I'd never get a win and I seriously began to consider packing in as I struggled over the mountain stages.

In the finishes the only rider fast enough and strong enough to help me was Sean. He was helping me get up and I was trying to rely on my speed in the last 100 metres but invariably there was never a way through. Fagor did get a stage win at Jaca in stage 12 when Sean clipped off on his own with Deno Davie on the run-in with about seven kilometres to go, and beat him by ten lengths in the sprint. But even that left a bit of a bad taste. As Sean crossed the line he made a sort of 'up yours' gesture – the Continental version of the V-sign. Of course this caused uproar among the Spaniards who probably all felt it was directed at them. In fact it was more like a gesture of relief, an easing of the frustration. He was saying: 'There you go, Fagor, I've won in spite of the way you're messing us about.'

Bazzo was furious, he went barmy. He thought it was an insult to all the spectators and demanded that Sean gave a press conference to explain. Perhaps he thought we were all going to get lynched. So Sean got up in front of the press and explained that back home it was a sign of elation and didn't mean anything and that he was sorry he had been misunderstood!

I still couldn't get near to Hermans in the sprints. At Albacete he actually fell off 1200 metres from the line, climbed back on and still won. They were all thinking thank God, he's gone, when he came steaming back up and went round them all.

Then, into Toledo, it finally clicked. Most of the ride from Albacete was uneventful. One rider got away with about 50 kilometres to go and was off on his own with a three-minute lead, but he came back gradually. In the last three miles the roads got quite hard with a climb to the finish through the walled gates of the city. This time the team were working their rocks off for me and Sean and Johnny Weltz both made big efforts to get me to the front. I could see the way they were going and I thought in panic, Christ, they're doing all this for me and I'm going backwards. I'm going to let them down.

Fortunately, just before the final pull, the road levelled out a bit and I began to get a second wind. In the last 800 metres I could see Millar going eyeballs out in front with Kelly glued to his wheel. It was quite a slow sprint, really, up the hill and on cobbles and I was in 53/18 which is a low gear for a sprint. I started fishing around, changed gears up and down a couple of times, then when I saw the banner I just gave it everything. I took so much out of the rest that they even gave me a time on them. It was my first win on the Continent.

Suddenly the sun had come out again. The hotel that night was a bit classy for a change and there was an English guy on reception to whom I was pleased to give a cycling cap. I rang home to tell my folks the news. It was a definite relief. I had been beginning to think there was a jinx on me. In the hotel my legs stopped hurting and I just felt so happy. My morale shot up as it always does after a victory and two days later I felt good enough to take on the race's top climbers. The stage finished with a really hard pull into Dyc and I actually stayed with the front group. A sprinter up there with Herrera, Cubino, Fuerte and Parra!

Bazzo, in the team car, couldn't believe it and sent Bagot, one of our guys, back to fetch me up. Just when I was beginning to think, this is it, I'll get over this climb and get them in the sprint, I hit a bump in the road and my back tyre blew. The service car was miles away so it took me about three minutes to get a wheel. That finished that. I know I could have won because all the other sprinters had been shelled out.

People have always classed me as a sprinter but nowadays I think I'm more complete than that. I prefer to think that I'll still be there at the end of a hard race when a lot of other sprinters have fallen by the wayside. You have to learn to hang in when things are getting really hard and then take the opportunities left when it gets flatter.

After the Vuelta I had seven weeks before the start of the Tour de France. I rode the Tour of Aragon, getting second in a mountain-top finish and winning the third stage before coming back to Britain for the National Championships in Newport, Shropshire.

I've never done well in the Nationals. Every time it's like chasing your own tail. The home pros see you and think, oh, here's Elliott and his big reputation, let's sort him out. I'm riding on my own and they're in teams and usually I get a really good working over. They make a conscious decision to try and take me down a peg or two. They don't want someone to come along and look too classy. They don't want to read in the papers that so-and-so returned from the Continent and gave the home pros a lesson.

A similar thing happened in the Tom Simpson Memorial race after the 1989 Tour of Spain. I got a real hammering. And, true to past form, finished eighth in the Nationals, feeling stale and a bit down. I knew by then that Roche was extremely doubtful for the Tour after his knee operation. Fagor were going into cycling's greatest challenge without a leader on the road.

8. Another Bloody Tour

With Roche out, Fagor at least stopped putting pressure on us. There were a few strong individuals in the team like Millar, Johnny Weltz and myself, but we all knew we weren't going to take the Tour de France by storm. With Roche gone, Millar was our nominal leader but by his own confession he wasn't going there to win it or even to get a place on the podium, so we were fairly relaxed about what was required of us. I knew it was going to be a bit of a struggle, a long month, and again I didn't set out with the total conviction that I was going to finish. It's just too much to stomach, the thought of being on your bike for 21 days. My approach was: maybe I'll get through a week, then I'll take it day by day.

The Tour began at Pontchâteau on 4 July with a 100-kilometre stage in the morning and a team time trial in the afternoon. It just didn't seem like the Tour de France. It had rained heavily the day before and it was really overcast on the start day. I remember talking to Paul Sherwen, the Channel Four commentator at the start-line and we remarked that the atmosphere just didn't seem like the Tour. It was cloudy and cold and I'd got a cape in my pocket. The cape went on and off and on again. Then the race was held up by a demonstration for 15 minutes and we got even colder.

Once we got going there were nervous riders everywhere,

pushing and shoving and trying to move up. It became a constant fight just to hold a place in the line and that was tiring in itself. In a situation like that the race can pass you by. I was well down the line when Steve Bauer, the guy I'd beaten for Commonwealth gold, went away strongly into the press motor bikes, so strongly that he took them by surprise. I never saw him go and when we came into the finish, I still had the idea we were sprinting for the win.

The last 300 metres of any sprint are weird. Everything goes very quiet and the riders seem to go into semi-trance. You're fully aware of what's happening but when you cross the line you feel as if you've suddenly woken from a dream. You can't recall details of where people were, who they were, how fast they were going or whether they were going faster than you. What I do know is that Hermans was glaring and moaning at me afterwards, like a disappointed child claiming I'd boxed him in. It was so ridiculous because if he was boxed in, so was I, and neither of us were going anywhere.

Sean, John Carlsson and myself were going really strong in the team time trial in the afternoon, probably too strong. The key to a team time trial is smoothness because you can't have one guy giving it everything and leaving gaps behind which the others can't fill. When Sean, John or myself got on the front, our efforts were greater. As we went into the lead the tempo would rise, but we had to be careful to wind it up gradually instead of getting in front and going bang!

At night there wasn't much Bazzo could say in the team talks. He would talk about the next day so that we knew where we were going. We were getting a fair battering and there was nothing he could come up with to ease the situation. I remember Sean telling me about the previous year when he'd raced 20 days in June and when it came to the Tour he got a real hiding. Bazzo scratched his head and said: 'Why are we getting such a battering? I know! We haven't raced enough, we haven't had enough preparation!' That was how much he knew about it!

After the Nantes to Le Mans stage Bazzo and Gomez demonstrated the extent of their cycling knowledge in no uncertain way. It was a really dodgy finish through the streets of Le Mans and we all came down together, going so fast. I had a job getting up near the front and an even bigger job staying there. Under the red kite, with a kilometre to go, there was a 90-degree left then a virtual 180-degree right. Going round these corners I lost a load of places – there were kamikazes coming from every direction. Sean came past me to try and take me up but I was absolutely nailed. He came up alongside and looked at me as if to say: 'Well, are you coming or not?' but I couldn't go with him.

Eventually I recovered a little, got the bike on to the 12 sprocket and started flying. From about 20 places back I got up to eighth at the line. When I got back to the hotel Bazzo and Gomez were there saying: 'What are you playing at Malcolm? You were the fastest over the last 300 metres by a mile.' They'd seen it on TV and watched me storming up to the barrier. 'Why didn't you get yourself nearer the front at the start of the sprint – Sean was there to help you, he could have taken you up.'

But it's not as simple as that: you go through patches, like the time into Toledo in the Tour of Spain. You go through one patch when you are actually going backwards then you get a second wind but just at the wrong time. I couldn't have moved up, but Bazzo and Gomez just didn't understand that.

That stage was the first of four for Jean-Paul Van Poppel, whose Dutch SuperConfex team dominated the flat stages. They always go into the Tour without an overall winner but the whole team are drilled to win stages. I've often thought what I could do with a team like that, but even with such a team, winning wouldn't come easy at first. You need experience of winning and there's a hell of a lot of pressure on you when there's a whole team riding for you in a finish and you fail to come up wth the goodies. I don't like that sort of pressure. Nor does it work every time. It can lead you to make mistakes.

When there's a rider appointed to lead you out in every sprint, like Sean for example, you have to follow him. You can't follow your instincts, you have to follow his and his instincts might take you well away from everybody to one side. So after he's died you're stuck out there on your own when you'd be better tucked away in a little knot of riders that can give you an easy ride before you nip past with a few metres to go.

On the third day there was a big crash on the road from Le Mans to Evreux. It happened just in front of me but I managed to get round the tangle. I thought, great, that's weeded a few of them out, but my problems were not yet over.

Having looked at the race map the night before I had the finish imprinted on my mind: round the last corner, a little climb, then down the descent and a 90-degree left over a bridge, then the finish. What the map didn't show was the nasty climb to the line. Over the bridge I took one look up the last drag and started searching for a wheel to get me up the hill. That's when Acacio Da Silva and Henri Abadie attacked and I cracked on the climb. On the line Da Silva put his hands in the air and nearly got caught by Rooks. For a long time no one knew who had won. Kelly, Da Silva's Kas team leader, was going barmy, saying: 'If he's lost that through putting his hands in the air I'll bloody well kill him!' I think he would have as well, because Kelly always claimed he backed off to give Da Silva the win.

The next day I missed the big break into Lièvin and immediately sank into the mid-Tour blues. It's always about that time, in the first ten days, that I get really depressed. I think I'd rather be doing anything but this – wouldn't it be good if I got sick and could jack it in! The thing is that if you jack it in for no good reason they could say you were in breach of contract. So all you can do is carry on and hope things get better. But that's when your mind starts straying and you're homesick and brassed off and wish you'd stayed a mechanic in a bike shop.

At Lièven, near the border with Belgium, Sean had his big day in the individual time trial. I could tell the night before that he was building up to something. The time trial was a bit of a target for him. I was planning to give it a good go and we were saying to each other: 'Well, am I going to beat you to the win, or are you going to beat me?' I was ahead of him overall and we made a joke of it. I said: 'You'll have to move over me tomorrow, Sean, or you'll never catch me.'

In the end he produced an unbelievable ride. If he'd finished in the first six it would have been a good ride but to slaughter that field in such a way left us all stunned. Lubberdink, the yellow jersey, was last man off and Breukink second. Conditions got worse for them as a bit of a wind blew up for the later starters but it makes no difference. Yatesy won and beat all these blokes, the best in the world.

The team management were patting themselves on the back, saying: 'Jolly good ride', as if in some way it was down to them. We always call Sean 'The Beast' and I shared a room with him, but I said to him jokingly after the stage: 'I don't want to share with you any more. You're too much of an animal – you frighten me!'

On the stage from Nancy to Strasbourg I was nearly wiped out by one of the perennial perils of the Tour de France. There were two hard climbs near the finish – short and not enough to split the field. But enough to string them out – and on the first climb I hit a guy with a movie camera. All the spectators had spilled out into the middle of the road and this prat was left standing right in front of the bunch. I tried to duck round him but clipped him and sent him and his camera flying. I hurt my shoulder and was left behind when Herrera attacked on the second climb and took a group clear. I was then left in the bunch behind on the descent and finished up kicking myself for not taking a bit more notice.

Belfort to Besançon was my last chance for a stage win before the race hit the Alps and I joined the 'laughing group' again. A lot of the other sprinters were obviously thinking the same because the driving finish was as fast as anything I'd been in. I got over the big climb of the Ballon de Servance better than I'd done in the whole race but I was disappointed when it all came back together to a bunch sprint again. With 200 metres to go I felt as though I'd got it, but that sprint was so fast – about 50 miles an hour – downhill and with a tailwind. The 53x12 I had on just wasn't big enough and Van Poppel, Bontempi, Planckaert and Dominguez all finished ahead.

The Alps are picturesque enough for tourists but to me they're just a bloody nuisance, something you've got to put up with, get over and hope that they will weed out some of the opposition. I'd be suffering as we climbed up them and be saying to myself: 'If Van Poppel and Planckaert or Hermans pack in over this, that will be nice!' I suppose it's quite an event, riding up Alpe d'Huez. Think about all the blood and guts that have been spilled there! But it's hard to take in the sheer size and duration of a mountain like that. Twenty kilometres of climbing! It's mind-boggling to sit and think about it, never mind get on a bike and ride it.

The Grenoble to Villard de Lans time trial will stick in most people's minds for all the wrong reasons. This was the day the yellow jersey was accused of doping. By the time we'd finished in the Alps, Delgado had seen off people like Bernard, Mottet and Fignon, all the French hopes, and was well on his way to victory. He'd been proved the best man, just as Roche had been the previous year. In the peloton there are always rumours and hearsay that all the top riders are positive and they are allowed to get away with it. I try to ignore it.

In 1987, when I came tenth at Troyes, the stage winner, Guido Bontempi, was found positive with testosterone, which is a banned hormone but which is present in your body anyway. What the authorities do is decide on a natural level and put a margin on top of that and anything over it is positive. Bontempi was declassified and lost the stage but it really didn't make any odds to me – it just meant I finished ninth instead of tenth. There were still eight others between me and him and I didn't feel cheated in any way. Bontempi's a great sprinter and a real animal, with or without testosterone.

In the 1988 Tour, Gert-Jan Theunisse of PDM was done for the same thing. He was supposed to have taken testosterone. He denied this, claiming that the results showed only his natural level, but since he's never been positive either before or since that really doesn't make sense.

There's a lot of confusion about doping in cycling and the Delgado affair was a classic example. If there is a positive test, the rider can ask for a counter test, and nothing is supposed to come out until that one, too, is proved positive. In Delgado's case there was a discrepancy. He was found positive the first time on something that wasn't a banned substance at the time and the second test was negative. The first Delgado knew about it was when a journalist told him at his hotel in Bordeaux, three days after the Villard de Lans time trial. That just wasn't on and a lot of the riders were annoyed about it.

At the start of the 19th stage from Clermont Ferrand to Chalon, the commissaire waved the race off and nobody moved. I saw some riders sit down at the front and this move gradually spread backwards like a wave until we were all sitting down in the road. Eventually the word got back that it was a protest about the way the Delgado affair had been handled. We were incensed that the press knew about the test result before the riders. It was totally out of order.

The other big drama in the 1988 Tour came on the Blagnac to Guzet-Neige stage, a mountain finish at a ski resort 1,500 metres up on the Pyrenees. Of course, it had to be a Fagor rider who suffered. Robert Millar had had an eminently forgettable Tour up to that point, but this was to finish him off. Millar has always gone well on the Pyrenees, though, and in 1983 and 1984 he'd had stage wins there. His 1984 win was in fact at Guzet-Neige. Unfortunately for him, they'd moved the finish for 1988.

As always in the mountains, the race up front had passed me by, as though it was a different event altogether, and it wasn't until we got to the hotel that we heard he'd come second, which was great. I remember saying: 'Who won it, then' and somebody told me that it was Massimo Ghirotto. I knew then that there was something wrong because Ghirotto is built bigger than me and there was no way he could win a mountain stage.

It turned out that Ghirotto, Millar and Philippe Bouvatier were approaching the finish together and winding up for the sprint when they came to the deviation for the team cars. There was one gendarme standing there and he wasn't particularly clear with his signals. Bouvatier and Millar followed the cars down the deviation, leaving Ghirotto, who'd been dropped, to carry on and take the stage. As soon as he realized what had happened Millar turned round and sprinted after him, but it was too late.

It was an absolute disaster for Millar because he always claimed he was on top of the gear, and felt he was going to win it. Then it was made even worse when a car was given to Bouvatier for a 'consolation prize' . . . and he'd come third! Millar took it very well considering; he was very philosophical about it. The way he was going, a second was a good result, but three days later at Limoges he climbed off and out of the Tour. Officially, he had a stomach complaint but after Guzet-Neige, where he had driven the break for most of the day, and been robbed of a victory, his morale must have cracked completely.

Fagor were going down like flies by then. We'd lost Eddy Schepers early on, then Pedro Munoz and Charly Berard. Bernard Richard packed in the day after Millar. Five down and four to go. The racing was harder than 1987 and I'm sure if it had been the 1988 race in 1987 I'd have gone too. It was just that I was one year more experienced and I'd learned some of the art of finishing. I was no nearer to winning a stage, though, and the Bordeaux third place in 1987 was still the nearest I'd been.

In 1988, each time I hit the front I knew from the way I was going that there was no conviction there, that I was going to get swamped. I hit the front in Paris on the last day for a while but my legs were folding and people were going to come back. Into Paris I'd been in a break that had been looking useful for a time and a lot of people said afterwards: 'You'd have done better in the sprint if you hadn't had to work in that break.' But it doesn't always work like that. Sometimes I can ride a race and be attacking all day and still feel good at the end. I get used to the continual effort. So when Sean led me out down the Champs-Elysées I was still feeling strong. With 100 metres to go I hit the front up the inside but Van Poppel appeared from nowhere again for his fourth stage win.

That guy amazes me. The Tour de France is his only target through the year. You don't hear or see anything of him and then he just turns it on, like a light switch, for the Tour. It has become almost mechanical for him.

I'd missed out on a stage win, but I'd come out of it without wrecking myself and in good shape. The temptation was to go out and belt a few beers back and relax for a couple of weeks, but I reasoned to myself: 'Hang on a bit, don't go daft, you can use this fitness for the Tour of Britain. You can win that.' I thought when I got back for the Kellogg's I was going as well as I ever had. Roche was back in the team, too, and with Millar, Yates and Bernard Richard completing the Fagor line-up, and with most of the week-long race on familiar ground, I knew I was in with a real chance.

9.   Crackle, Pop and Snap

The images most cycling fans will remember of the 1988 Kellogg's Tour of Britain are the sight of the red and white jerseys of Fagor controlling the race from the front, going at it hammer and tongs with no one else able to get in attacks. With me in yellow from day one, all the team worked like machines to protect me. It was, as they said on Channel Four, a really professional team performance. How professional, people will never appreciate, because backstage the team set-up hardly existed. The team that Stephen Roche had handpicked was breaking apart. On the road there was plenty of crackle and pop, but behind the scenes things were about to snap.

Looking around the Kellogg's field, I considered the main danger would come from Joey McLoughlin and his Z-Peugeot team. He was fresh from a season free of the Milk Race and a Tour de France and was the defending champion, although it takes a lot to win a race two years running. Kelly was there with Kas, but I think he knew he didn't have the team to take an overall win.

I took the prologue in Newcastle by nine seconds from my old rival Mark Walsham and won another five seconds on the road from Newcastle to York by taking Hotspot sprints. Then we hit the climbs. Over the moors of North Yorkshire, the field had been whittled down to 15 in front when we hit Rosedale Chimney. I recall two or three of us getting detached at the bottom of the hill but I just relaxed and tried to keep an even tempo going.

People rave about the climbs in the Alps but this is really something else. I looked up and I could see the crowd lining the road from left to right until we turned one corner and there was a stream of people going literally straight up the hill in one continuous line. They looked as if they were standing in a field and I thought, where the hell does the road go? Riders were off their bikes, walking, and the road went straight up this one-in-three funnel. The looks on the faces of some of the foreign riders were a picture. When I got on it I felt as if I was going to roll over backwards. I had a 39x24 gear on, which is low, very low, and I was on the verge of coming to a complete halt – if I'd gone any slower I'd have stopped – when it eased very gently and the worst was over.

At the top we had a 75-mile run-in to York and Mauro Gianetti of the Swiss Weinmann team clipped off straight away. We regrouped and with Millar, Yates and Roche working, keeping the pace at the front high, we tore into York. The stage finished with a few laps round the city and Thomas Wegmüller of Kelly's Kas team got away, while Kelly, behind him, as any good team rider would do, slowed us all down by getting in our way on the corners. In the last kilometre there were two or three more 90-degree bends and that's when I decided I had to go because everyone else was looking at each other and wondering who was going to bring Wegmüller back. Kelly tried to lean on me and we banged into each other but I got away with Joey on my right. The next corner was a left 90 degrees and I held the inside line. I went crazy round that corner and Joey had to drop off because it looked suicidal. With 130 metres to go, Wegmüller was six lengths up but I gave it everything and sneaked over him with what must have been a ten-foot lunge.

The next day into Manchester stirred up some controversy, with Joey at the centre of it. Over Shibden Wall and Holme Moss the race had been whittled down to 20 or so, with other riders shelled out all over the place. The last 15 miles were a circuit of the city and, of course, as the later arrivals got on to the circuit we were lapping them. They were all over the place and should have been pulled out by the commissaire because they started getting in everyone's way. As Joey led the sprint out I was baulked but got back up when we got to the last corner where Joey cut across me and went like stink the last few yards to win.

I wasn't too upset after two stage wins already and it wasn't entirely illegal what he'd done – if you can get away with it then you do. I had to back off, otherwise I'd have finished among the flowerpots they had adorning the finish area, and if it hadn't been the flowerpots it would have been the fence and the crowds. Joey is a friend as well as a rival and the fact that he'd had a poor season up until then meant I didn't begrudge him the win.

Serge Demierre of Weinmann got away on stage three from Manchester to Liverpool but we weren't really too bothered. He was a long way down overall and we figured that with a rider off the front it would neutralise the race. People would be looking at Fagor to bring him back and we could ride at our own tempo. At one time he had about 18 minutes and we had a discreet word with his Weinmann team-mates to say that we wouldn't bring him back, would leave him out there as long as he posed no threat to me, but for that we'd expect help from them later on if it was needed. They agreed, Demierre got the stage and the glory and kept the Weinmann sponsors happy. We got the promise of help if the going got tough.

At the time the television coverage was making a lot of Roche and his comeback race and the cameras were on him much of the time. So when Roche attacked to cover another rider – went over him and formed a strong-looking break with Keith Reynolds and Mike Doyle – there was a lot of speculation that he was actually attacking me, his team-mate and race leader. At the time I was just happy to see a rider from my team in front and to see the Peugeot riders having to do some work. It was lifting our riders. It's like a game of chess: you move your pieces up one by one. If Roche had won the stage and taken the jersey we'd have been first and second. If someone else had won, we'd have been third or fourth. Roche's attack might have cost me the race, but you can't be selfish about these things.

Roche figured in another incident which probably baffled a lot of television viewers during that same stage when we got near Clitheroe in North Lancashire. It's the home town of Allan Gornall and as they so often do in the Tour de France, it was agreed he could ride on ahead and say hello to his family and friends. No one would chase him. Gornall clipped off and we let him go, but then having got through Clitheroe he carried on riding instead of sitting up and coming back to the bunch. He got three or four minutes up and of course that was breaking one of the unwritten rules of cycling. When we eventually got him back he said: 'I waited for ages and ages and I was getting cold so I just rode on.' It took us about ten miles to catch him so he must have warmed up all right!

The first to get to him was Roche who gave him a right bollocking which was captured on television. (Less well-informed viewers couldn't understand the etiquette of a race where one rider is allowed to ride away for personal reasons and then supposed to stop and rejoin the bunch.) The cameras kept showing Roche hanging on to the car door, taking phone calls and they must have thought, what's going off here – they're supposed to be racing and there's one guy on the telephone all the time!

It was turning into quite an eventful race. I wasn't going for stage wins any more, just defending the jersey, and keeping Joey off my back. Fagor and Yates the Beast were overpowering everyone.

On stage five, Birmingham into Bristol, Henri Abadie got away on his own and became leader on the road for a time, but Fagor pulled him back. Yates, Roche and Millar were all riding as if it was a team time trial, and it was a great effort – particularly by Yates who hardly ever got off the front – but backstage all wasn't sweetness and light. Among the riders there was no animosity, it was just that Fagor were such difficult people to deal with. The team began to fall apart.

Yates had decided he was going anyway. He wanted to go to a team that had a different mentality. He'd always ridden with French teams and was tired of their traditional approach. He just needed a fresh start and figured he could get that with an American team. With Millar, things were a bit murkier. He'd been in dispute with Mondragon because he hadn't been paid all year. For the first six months of the year neither had I, but at least I got my salary in June – the first money I'd had from them. Millar didn't get a cent until September. He had a solicitor working on Mondragon but basically he wasn't too bothered. He'd had a bellyful of Fagor and he thought if they hadn't paid him he could do them for breach of contract and tear it up and get out. He had a two-year deal with them and wanted freedom from it. But he finished up losing that one, too. There were rumours that he'd already signed for Peugeot and Fagor took their complaint to the UCI. Millar was fined £45,000 for breach of contract. It was all a bit confusing but then so are a lot of things that go in European cycling. A lot of decisions are made and judgements passed that have ulterior motives behind them.

Another example was the occasion in Lièvin during the 1988 Tour de France when Fagor announced in *L'Equipe* that Stephen had signed a new three-year contract with them, which would take him to the end of his career, virtually. Apparently Mondragon had taken him on one side and told him: 'Tell the world you've signed for another three years or Fagor will sue you. I'll sue for defamation of character and for taking all that money off us and not riding.' So Roche made the announcement. At the time Roche and Valcke were working on putting together a new team and when Valcke heard the news about the Fagor deal it made him ill. He thought that the work they'd done had gone to waste. He was taken to hospital – there was something wrong with his heart.

That night in Lièven, Stephen arrived and told us the full story; that he hadn't actually signed for three years, he'd had a gun put to his head. All the riders understood, except Pedro Munoz who is Spanish and seemed to have a foot in both camps. Munoz was with Fagor long before Roche and Valcke came along and he always held an opposing view. There was some animosity there, too. After the Semaine Catalan back in March, Munoz went on to the Criterium International and packed in on the first day. Valcke had a real go at him in front of everybody: 'If you're going to pack in on the first day you shouldn't have come at all, you should have let someone else have a go.' When we'd voted to keep Crepel, Munoz had had his reservations. He was getting a lot of money from Fagor and it was in his interests not to be too contrary with them.

In many ways at that time it was a relief to get out on the road in the mornings and away from the politics.

When we came into London and the last one-mile circuit around Westminster I was again in a position where I had to fall off or puncture to lose it. In the event there was a crash, but well away from me and again Joey had to carry the can. There had been some dark mutterings about Joey's riding throughout, but this time I voted him 'not guilty'.

On the last corner Jacques Hanegraaf of the Toshiba team took off and Johann Lammerts, seeing this, decided to close things down for his team-mate. He took the corner fairly narrow then swung out wide so that nobody could come round and Hanegraaf would have a clear run to the line. Joey was on his outside and flicked outwards, causing a twitch that was passed down the line. Mark Walsham was on the end of that line and it was like being on the end of a whip, he went out and hit a lamp-post solid. I stayed out of the mêlée and went over the line to take the second Kellogg's Tour of Britain and a Citroën BX19 GTI. Being a team effort, this was immediately sold off and the cash split between the Fagor riders.

The Tour of Britain win finished off what I would call an average year with Fagor. I'd had the win in the Tour of Spain but had missed out in France. Would Fagor want me for 1989? I wanted away from them and I was always hopeful that Roche and Valcke were going to get their new team off the ground and I could be a part of it. They were talking with Bernard Tapie, once the owner of Bernard Hinault's team La Vie Claire, and the owner of the Marseilles Football Club, but that eventually fell through.

Back in June, I'd packed in the Midi-Libre which really upset Bazzo and the rumour was that Fagor weren't going to renew my contract. Then, of course, I'd put on a bit of a show on the last stage of the Tour in Paris. Gomez and Mondragon were there and I was back in their good books. At two in the morning, after a meal in the Moulin Rouge, they'd started their overtures.

'We'll have a different *directeur sportif*, Malcolm,' Mondragon had said. 'We know you don't get on with Bazzo.'

'It's not that I don't get on with Bazzo – I just don't rate him as a manager,' I'd replied.

I knew then they were keen on re-signing me and the Kellogg's Tour would reinforce that. The only question was: For how long and for how much?

10. Viva Espana!

The official end of the cycling season for me is the Sun Tour of Victoria in Australia. It's a race with a holiday atmosphere and I can't wait for it, getting the last race in Europe out of the way and going out to Australia to enjoy a relaxing time. It's by invitation only and the Aussie professionals there are good, strong riders but with a more relaxed attitude than their European counterparts, which suits me, of course.

At the end of 1988, however, I still didn't have a job to return to. My contract with Fagor had expired and they were messing me about on renewing it. A couple of days before I set off to Australia I'd gone over to France to sign, but 30 miles from Dover I'd made a phone call and was told they hadn't got the contract ready yet, so I just turned round and went home again. When I set out for Australia I didn't know who I was riding for in 1989. After four days of the Sun Tour I was awakened in the middle of the night by the phone in my hotel room.

It was Phil Griffiths, the former *directeur sportif* of ANC. He was in Switzerland with Darryl Webster, the well-known British pro who was about to sign for the Spanish Team Teka, who manufacture domestic applicances. Phil is the UK agent for Assos, the clothing company, who have links with Teka through Tony Meier, the Assos boss man. Teka's general manager is Santiago Revuelta, who is a sort of Tony Capper of Spanish cycling, a man with his finger in everything, and Phil had casually mentioned to him that I was looking for a team and would they be interested? Teka obviously knew me from the Tour of Spain and said that they were interested. Phil asked me how much I wanted. I told him and he went back to Revuelta who said yes. All this was taking place over the phone between Switzerland and Australia in the middle of the night and I was bit dubious. Sitting in Australia at five in the morning on the end of a phone, with a guy I didn't know saying he was going to pay me so much for riding for his company seemed a bit hard to take in. I didn't immediately crack open the champagne. I was just waiting to see what happened when I got back home.

Within a week of getting back, Fagor were in touch. Could I meet Mondragon and Ramon Mendiburu, Fagor's new public relations man, at Heathrow Airport for 'a talk about the future'?

I arrived at the Holiday Inn at the airport and walked in to find Mondragon and Mendiburu sitting there . . . with Stephen Roche and Sean Kelly. Fagor were trying to get these two superstars in the same team and wanted me along, too. I knew what Roche and Kelly were worth, so obviously Fagor had upped their budget somewhat. Kelly at that time was talking to nine or ten teams so I wasn't overly surprised to see him there.

We didn't waste time on small talk; we all knew what we were there for but as the negotiations went on, it quickly became obvious that I was going nowhere. They'd been talking to Kelly and Roche and now they obviously thought, right, we've got this little nobody from Sheffield, we'll soon sort him out. They proposed to pay me the same as the year before but with a scale of bonuses – carrots to chase.

I said: 'Bonuses are all very well, but it's not money in your pocket.'

'That's what you're worth, that's what we're offering', said Mondragon. But I knew with the win in Spain and the Kellogg's Tour victory I had the bargaining power and we finished up in deadlock. What Fagor didn't know was that I held an ace up my sleeve in Teka, and two days later I flew out to Bilbao to meet their big noises.

I was picked up at the airport by Julio San Emeterio, the *co-directeur sportif* and driven to Santander to meet Gonzales Linares, the other *co-directeur* of the team. San Emeterio is a round bloke in his fifties with a pleasant, easy-going manner, a bit too soft really to be a *directeur sportif*. Linares, in contrast, is the craggy-faced, hard man. He bangs his fist on the table a lot, but he's an ex-rider, and a good rider, so he merited respect.

At Fagor, Bazzo just wasn't forceful enough. He couldn't jump up and down at a team meeting because there were riders there that he felt inferior to. There were a lot of individuals in the team and he was very cautious about telling them what they should do. He would suggest, rather than tell you, to do things. Linares would tell you something and as soon as he left the room it would be done. At Teka the riders are more like a bunch of soldiers, they do as they are told and are less individual in their thinking. They wouldn't, for example, take the mickey out of Linares as soon as his back was turned like they used to with Bazzo at Fagor. Not for the fear that it might get back to him, just because he might be right.

I met Revuelta and we sat down and went through a few things. Everything seemed bona fide but I wasn't swept off my feet by a slick professional set-up. It was as I expected a Spanish team to be, not particularly avant-garde in their thinking, not very progressive – they'd only change a system because everybdy else had changed. But Teka seemed an honest outfit and they genuinely seemed to want me. The money was right and they were not going to put pressure on me to live over there between races. I could return to Sheffield any time, so in many ways it was better for me personally than it would be at Fagor.

I'd bought a house in Sheffield by then and I wanted more time at home with my girlfriend Luci rather than spending half my year away.

I'd met Luci five years earlier in Fanny's nightclub in Sheffield and we had gradually become closer until we finished up under the same roof together. Luci is a 23-year-old model and photographic make-up artist, and it's become important for me now to arrive home and find her waiting for me.

Apart from Darryl Webster I knew Regis Clère at Teka from his amateur days in France and there was Peter Hilse who had ridden the Milk Race a few years previously and speaks good English. His fellow German and team leader was Raimund Dietzen who we were later to lose in a horrendous accident in the Tour of Spain.

It was 12.30 a.m. when we finished in Revuelta's office and I was exhausted but Teka must have sensed that I was close to signing because they took me out to a restaurant and wined and dined me until two. Revuelta phoned the restaurant especially and got it to stay open an extra two hours. That quite impressed me, too.

I went back to the hotel and thought, I've come all this way to Bilbao, everything looks good, what reason have I not to sign? I tried to phone Roche to explain but he was away in Munich. I tried to ring Valcke and he was on a *directeur sportif* course in Belgium. Then I phoned Mondragon. I didn't tell him where I was, just asked him: 'Have you had any second thoughts about your offer?'

'No, not really, we thought that was a good offer,' he replied.

'Right, I'm here in Spain and I'm going to sign for Teka.'

Mondragon went spare. 'Oh no, Malcolm, you shouldn't go

to them. They're an unreliable set-up. You can't trust them. You'll be sold up the river!'

I quite enjoyed that.

The next day I signed the contract with Teka and within two minutes a pressman just happened to appear, with a camera round his neck. I put on a Teka jersey that just happened to be lying around and the reporter took his picture. I asked him not to use it for a couple of days until I'd spoken to Roche or Valcke, but next day it was all over the paper, so that was how they found out. Roche was said to be upset about me walking out on Fagor, but I think he understands now that it was Fagor who were dragging their heels, messing me about.

Teka's first race was the Tour of the Americas which started in Venezuela and finished in Florida, with points from both counting for an overall title. Teka seemed to have the programme a lot better worked out than Fagor. I did as many races with them, but with a lot less travelling. With Fagor I was riding a one-day race, then had a huge drive and a two-day race somewhere else. With Teka I did the seven days of the Americas then came home. I rode the Paris-Nice straight through then came home. The same with the Semaine Catalan. That's better for me than filling in with a really hard race in Belgium that I couldn't finish anyway, 100 miles over cobbles with mud and water splashing in my face. That sort of thing just demoralises me.

A lot of the European teams were down in South America and it was quite an impressive field. There was PDM, Fagor, Chateau d'Ax. Reynolds were also there with Pedro Delgado and some of the Americans, including Greg Lemond. I liked the Tour of Americas. It was really hot and the terrain was a lot more interesting than Spain, although it's the first race I've been in anywhere where a stage was cancelled because of a riot. I've known stages re-routed or cut short for some reason – Het Volk was called off because of six foot snowdrifts four years ago – but never one cancelled for a riot.

A student had been shot by the police in Maracay, Venezuela, and there was some sort of mass protest to coincide with the third day of the Tour. The students had kidnapped the race commissaire and were holding him hostage. They'd lit big fires in the field by the finishing straight. The fire brigade and the police were there but as soon as they put one fire out the students would start another. They wouldn't release the commissaire either, and after about 40 minutes past the scheduled start the race jury decided to call it a day – they couldn't risk us flying up and down this road with stones whistling past our heads.

Like kids who get out of school early, there was a lot of cheering among the riders and there were smiles everywhere as we rode the 60 kilometres back to Valencia. Then on the road back it started chucking down with rain and about six or seven riders went down on an oil slick and cut themselves up pretty badly.

Back on the road, I did quite well. I was second in the first day from Valencia to Caracas when I rode, eyeballs out, up a couple of hard climbs near the end. I was suffering but it was a smooth sort of suffering and when Luis Herrera came past me, I was able to take his wheel to get back up.

With three second places on stages and second overall in the Tour of the Americas I was pleased with my early season form, but in the Paris-Nice the week after I was brought back down to earth. That was a hard race. I just couldn't get over some of the climbs and there were only two days in the whole race when I could honestly say I was competing – stage one where Etienne de Wilde won and on the last into Nice where I got second place to Adriano Baffi. But really I was relieved to miss the top 80 cut-off and the final time trial up the Col d'Eze. Peter Hilse was going well and Raimund Dietzen reasonably well but Regis Clère and I and the rest were in groups a long way down.

As for the Teka administration, it seemed to be the same old story – you had to sing for your salary.

In Venezuela I'd come across Patrick Valcke again who had been taken back into the Fagor camp as joint *directeur sportif* with Bazzo. And on the Paris-Nice I'd seen even more of him and the rest of the Fagor team. Naturally, they asked me if I was happy at Teka and I replied that things were OK. Then Valcke dropped his bombshell. He said: 'I could fix it for you to go back with Fagor.'

'But what about my contract with Teka?'

He said they could get me out of that, too, and if Teka took me to court Fagor would pay the compensation.

'I've seen Mondragon and he's great friends with the boss of Teka and will release you from the contract so that you can come and ride with us. Fagor will pay the same money as Teka, but there would also be a transfer fee for you.' Apparently Fagor needed my world-ranking points to stay in the top 20 of the team ratings and to keep getting invitations to the top races.

I was tempted. I'd missed some of the mates I'd made at Fagor and I'd keep running into their mechanics who'd say: 'Is that right, you're coming back to us?' By this time we were into March and I still hadn't been paid by Teka so I didn't feel a fantastic loyalty to them. But having worked with the people at Fagor in the past it sounded too dodgy for words. I had my reputation to think of, too, and after I'd taken some advice on it and let it ride, the affair gradually fizzled out.

My first win of the season came in the Semaine Catalan prologue the week after all the suffering in the Paris-Nice. The course was only two or three kilometres and when I saw it I thought, this is just like a Milk Race prologue, this will suit you down to the ground. I didn't say anything to anybody but I really fancied my chances. I rode round it five or six times, getting to know every bit of the circuit intimately and after I finished I knew no one could go faster on that course. In the end I won by six seconds, which is a hell of a lot on such a short course.

My confidence continued in the afternoon road race where I beat Hermans and the bunch in the sprint, and the day after I was third. I was going well. Then, as so often happens, bad luck took its turn. The finish was in Andorra and there was a first category climb five kilometres from the finish. I was dropped, but on the descent I was coming back on to the group when I punctured. I was just coming into a hairpin when I hit a lump in the road, the tyre burst and rode off all in the same motion and wrapped itself in a neat little knot round my back brake. In situations like that you don't think, you just act and I managed to slam on the front brake, stopping a couple of feet before a big drop down the other side of the road.

Marino Alonso, one of my team-mates, stopped and gave me his wheel. He had to walk back up the hill to me and I finished a minute down, dropping from first to 15th. I lost more time on a hilltop finish above Andorra the next day but at least Dietzen took over the jersey, and on the last day Hermans led me out in the last 150 metres and I went over him easily for my third win of the week.

So Dietzen won the race, I won the points and Teka took the team. It was a successful week all round. I could tell how happy Teka were because for the first time Linares agreed to take me to the airport. He didn't know the way and kept going wrong so I sat in the back with the race manual tucked out of sight on my knee – the manual happened to have Barcelona Airport on it – and directed him. He was amazed. 'You know Spain better than me!' he cried.

Teka did have some characters in that team. One of the biggest was Jaime, a *soigneur* with a huge Mexican moustache. A couple of years ago at the Teka team launch in some Marbella casino, Jaime got drunk and lost seven million pesetas, about £35,000, on the gaming tables. The casino was owned by Teka's top man, so at least the money went back into the team!

After Semaine Catalan it was back home and the Tour of North East Derbyshire which I rode in leg warmers, arm warmers and cape as it chucked it down all day. This produced an oddity, the lone Elliott break, as I went the last 15 miles on my own to win. My legs had gone, anyway, and I knew I wasn't going to win a sprint so I thought I'd just give it everything and if I was caught, too bad.

After rain in Derbyshire, it was snow in Spain at the Trophy Castilla Leon, a five-day stage race which had an overall win to go for, but on which you could stop any day you wanted and start again the next. On the first stage a level-crossing came down on us with three kilometres to go and the whole race stood there pushing and shoving while the train went past. It was one of those races . . . The next day it was white all over, with almost horizontal snow, and with 30 kilometres to go I got a puncture. I thought, great, now's my chance to get out, as I dropped back. But one of the riders must have seen me and three or four of them dragged me back, protesting, to get my wheel changed at the car. In the end I was glad they had helped because the effort of getting back up to the bunch shook off the lethargy and I began to feel stronger. Hilse led me out with 600 metres to go through the town and I went from the last corner to win by five lengths.

The next day was icy cold and they were going to take us into the mountains, so while the race headed for the hills I took the short cut home. They took the high road and I took

(*Above*) That bubbly feeling . . . a 1987 promotion for London City Airways.

(*Left*) Suffering for Fagor in the Tour of Spain, 1988. (*Graham Watson*)

At last . . . victory at Toledo in the 1988 Tour of Spain, with Sean Kelly beaten.

Olé! A salute for the fans in Toledo.

The price of fame . . . tired or not, a rider must do his duty to the media. (*Graham Watson*)

(*Left*) I should have brought a brolly . . . victory in a very rainswept Tour of north-east Derbyshire. (*Paul Ibberson*) (*Right*) But everyone else got wet, too. (*Paul Ibberson*)

(*Left*) Back on my home patch in Sheffield wearing the Tour of Spain points jersey. (*Paul Ibberson*)

(*Below*) In the Tom Simpson Memorial race with Jon Walshaw. (*Paul Ibberson*)

Tour of Spain, 1989 – it's lovely, this winning! (*Graham Watson*)

Another stage win in Spain's Tour of Burgos, 1989. (*Gianfranco Soncini*)

(*Above*)   Words of advice from my Teka *directeur sportif* at Manchester Piccadilly during the 1989 Kellogg's Tour of Britain. (*Simon Pendrigh*)

(*Left*)   A rare moment of relaxation with the girl in my life, Luci. (*Simon Pendrigh*)

(*Opposite, above left*) Superman . . . Jean-Paul Van Poppel. (*Graham Watson*)

(*Above right*)   Motorman . . . Guido Bontempi in the Paris-Roubaix. (*Graham Watson*)

(*Below*)   Hermans gets his own back in the 1989 Tour of Spain. (*Graham Watson*)

Friendly rival . . . Hermans, ready for combat with me in the 1989 Tour of Spain. (*Graham Watson*)

Patrick Valcke and Stephen Roche. (*Graham Watson*)

the low road and I was in Segovia before them. Linares wasn't too pleased about that, but the next day at Zamora there was another bunch sprint and I won that, leading out from 200 metres and sticking my elbows out so that no one could get past.

A second place behind Jorge-Manuel Dominguez on the last day put me in good heart for the Tour of Spain and I bypassed the Teka training camp – what Linares liked to call the 'concentration' and headed home.

The day before the 1989 Vuelta I was in bed in La Coruna with a streaming cold and a sore throat. The Teka doctor came in to see me two or three times a day in an effort to get me fit for the prologue on the Monday. In situations like that you have to be very careful what you take. Some so-called cold cures have trace elements that could make you positive in a dope test, and when a rider gets sick he needs good medical advice from someone who's also aware of what you can and can't take.

The Tour produced some epic sprinting battles between me, Mathieu Hermans and Eddy Planckaert with, since I finished with the points jersey, the honours definitely going to M. Elliott. The first stage proper was a monster 209 kilometres from La Coruna to Santiago de Compostella and I got fourth when three riders got 50 metres on us and I didn't quite have it to get across to them. A blown opportunity, really, but at least Hermans and Planckaert had finished about 9 and 16 minutes down. Things went better the next day.

After a team time trial in the morning, I sensed that in the afternoon stage from Vigo to Orense it was going to be a really good day. I felt so strong. It was an uphill finish and I came from a long way back, passing riders. It was that which kept me going. The last two riders I reached were Planckaert and his ADR team-mate Marnix Lamiere, his lead-out man.

Planckaert took me all over the road, right over to the barrier and I think he thought I'd back off but I kept going, and as soon as I got in front I went back at him. If I hadn't won I'd have put a protest in. That day started the needle between myself and him because I went on television and in pidgin Spanish said that what he'd done had been on the edge of legitimacy. But Planckaert knew what he'd done and I was just making it clear that I knew, too. Planckaert got his win a couple of days later and Hermans, who'd won six stages the year before, was starting to sweat a bit.

Into Toledo, where I'd had my win in the Fagor jersey in 1988, Massimo Ghirotto – Millar's mate from Guzet-Neige – went from a really long way out and just sort of hung there. Then Hermans went and I was on his wheel, but he got the second place, the first time he'd really shown on the Tour. The previous year he'd looked invincible, but he hadn't seemed any sort of threat this year. On the stage that I won he wasn't even in the first ten.

A couple of days later I clashed with Planckaert again. One of the Once riders had got away and won by a good distance so we were sprinting for second place. Planckaert was in front and I came up behind him, giving him plenty of room, but as I went past he just went, wham!, and smacked into my handlebars. I had to stop completely and finished seventh. But this time I did protest, Planckaert was disqualified and I moved up a place keeping my grip on the blue points jersey. At least he had the grace to apologise later when he said: 'I didn't see you there!'

I took my third Tour of Spain stage victory into Lerida after a day when most of the teams were content to keep things together, knowing it was a good day for the sprinters. It was a slightly uphill finish, sweeping round a right-hand corner, and everything went perfectly. I got into the right place, where I wanted to be, with the road clear in front and went across Planckaert to win. He got second.

86

Winning in Spain is a chaotic business. The public are over the top in everything. Kids are demanding 'Give us your hat', and trying to grab something, anything, off you. As soon as you cross the line they stick a television camera up your nose. But that day it was all worth it. The only disappointing thing was the reaction of the British press. There wasn't one British reporter on the race and most of them back home didn't realise I was in the points jersey until I returned. But then compared with the Tour de France, the Vuelta has a bit of a reputation for being stark. No freebies, no wining and dining. The journalists just don't want to know.

After Lerida, Hermans seemed to get a second wind and took two stage wins. I started to do some mental arithmetic, trying to figure out what I'd have to do to keep the points jersey. I thought what if I don't score any points in the last couple of days and Hermans carries on finishing like he has been doing? I was definitely starting to panic.

Valladolid was the big test because after that there was only a time trial and a mountain stage before we finished in Madrid. In the end I got a second at Valladolid but the finish didn't come a second too soon because I got sick with a day to go – a recurrence of the bug I'd had before the start of the tour – and it was only aspirins that kept me alive on the last stage. They wore off towards the finish and I just rode in wrecked, in tenth place to clinch the points victory. There was no celebrating, though. I left that night for Sheffield. I'd been away for almost three weeks and I just wanted to get home.

The Friday after the Tour de Spain I took part in a criterium in York and I rode the tyre off on the last corner. My mechanic had failed to glue it on properly and it just rolled straight off. I took a flyer and got cut up a bit, but it wasn't that which bothered me. It was the thought that I'd been doing all those hairy descents in Spain a week earlier on the same bike prepared by the same mechanic. It brought home to me what a fine line there is in cycling between glory and disaster.

11. Tumbled

The spectre of serious injury or worse is always there in cycling. And if you don't get floored by a fall or an accident there's always the fear of a stress-related injury. It was the last weekend in May after the near miss at York that I noticed a dull ache just above my right knee. I was riding the Tour of Astorias and the pain started midway through the first stage. In situations like these most teams are fairly sympathetic so there were no objections from the Teka management when I climbed off on the second day, unwilling to risk possible long-term damage. I saw doctors and specialists who were unable to diagnose what was wrong in the thigh and I carried on trying to rest it whenever possible.

Dietzen, the Teka team leader, was still seriously ill in hospital so in many ways it was a relief that we didn't get an invitation to the Tour de France. In France I would have suffered with the knee, I know. I would have been seriously disadvantaged. Still, I tried to carry on with a combination of rest and light training until I rode the Tour of Wales where I had to stop on the last day with a searing pain so bad that I could hardly bend my leg. I began to get seriously worried.

Cyclists are insured against injury ending their careers but it's very hard to quantify what would be considered serious enough. If you make a claim obviously you can't start riding again, and claims can take months to investigate while the insurers decide whether you are bad enough to be written off. In the end I went down to London to see a specialist called Frank Westall and he diagnosed the problem in a flash. The musculature round the base of my pelvis was out of line and it was throwing everything else out down the thigh. Two days later I was riding in the National Championships, coming 14th with barely a twinge. The scare was over, but I'd been sweating for a time. As I've said before, cycling is like being on a tightrope. One minute you're on top of the world and the next you could be in a hospital bed. It's a short career and a dangerous one and you have to learn to look after number one.

'Elliott in dispute over Kellogg's fee', said the newspaper headlines as the countdown began for the defence of the Tour of Britain yellow jersey. It was true, there was a dispute and some ill-feeling at the time. It upset me a lot and I believe it coloured the coverage I got when the Tour actually started. I was the previous year's winner, but you'd hardly have thought so. In all the pre-race posters there was no picture of me, nothing in the programme or TV Times and when I won the prologue by a crushing margin, a margin so wide that officially eight other riders were eliminated for finishing too far adrift, it was hardly mentioned.

What happened was simple: for the first time I asked for an appearance contract for the Kellogg's. Someone like Kelly negotiates an appearance fee for every race he's in, judging quite rightly that his name and presence are going to create more interest and put bums on seats. As defending champion, I felt the same. I felt I was a pull for the Tour organisers, but we were miles apart on what they were offering me and what I thought I was worth. I think they thought I would have a moral obligation as a Briton to turn up and try and keep the jersey for my country. Part of me felt that way, but I was also going to make sure they didn't use me. So the sparring started. First of all I announced I wouldn't be riding and tried to put it behind me. I didn't want to bury the idea and I wanted Teka to think I was still going. Faxes flashed back and forth between Britain and Spain. Teka got the team contract to sign and I told them: 'Don't whatever you do put my name on the contract, just say five riders and leave it at that.'

All the time the race was getting nearer and nearer. It was like a balancing act. I wanted to ride it because I enjoy racing in Britain and I wanted to show up with a good Teka team, but I wasn't going to be sold short. Eventually we agreed on a contract and I could get down to the riding again, but as I say it left some ill-feeling. I became so paranoid about it that when I looked at the prologue and saw the steepness of the climb I thought, bastards! They've picked this one to make sure I don't have a chance!

Kelly has the wheeler-dealing off to a tee and was obviously happy with what he got, but Roche had found the organisers' offer laughable and turned them down flat. Of the other riders, Martin Earley probably got a cut from Kelly as his team-mate. I don't think Bob Millar got a bean which really choked him off.

The hardest parts of the Kellogg's Tour of Britain are the lengths of the stages and the smallness of the teams. So much is left to chance and with only five men in a team it's very hard to control a race. Of course, you'd never find a team so strong and so in control as Fagor the year before, but with Millar, Roche and Sean Yates riding as my domestiques, I think you could call that a one-off.

In 1989 I had a good team, with Peter Hilse and Marino Sanchez as the leading characters and I couldn't have improved on the riders Teka had available, particularly as they had to send men to the Tour of Catalan the same week. The danger I saw as Kelly and Millar although in San Sebastian on 12 August Millar had said he didn't want to ride the Kellogg's. He was miffed because he had four criteriums in France lined up for the same week with a lot more money on offer than the Kellogg's but Z-Peugeot, his team, were making him go. Even when he got to Britain he was talking about riding a couple of days then climbing off and heading back home to Troyes. In the light of what was to happen over the Tumble on the stage into Cardiff, maybe he was trying a bit of 'kidology'!

The prologue climb up to Dundee's landmark – the Law – was supposed to be two and a half miles but after a couple of rides up it the day before the race began, it struck me that the climb seemed very short, over very quickly. Someone told me they had measured it at 1.8 miles and I began to feel a bit more optimistic. Everything went right. I was last off and the times of the earlier riders were all around six minutes so I knew they'd measured the course wrong. At the start I felt relaxed and dreamlike, almost in a trance. Looking back I think I could have gone harder, though at the finish when I came in first a lot of people thought I'd gone over the top because the cameras caught me flat on my back gasping for air and to all appearances wrecked. I had to put up with a few jibes from my fellow riders about 'the Oscar-winner' and Joey McLoughlin kept saying: 'Spielberg's been on the phone for you again, Malc', but there were no seats and no catchers at the finish line and I just had to flop down somewhere – the road was the only place.

So, like 1988, I was in yellow on the first day and a marked man. Stage one was to take us 117 miles from Dundee to Glasgow, and Kelly and Martin Earley, with the help of a steady downpour set out to destroy me. Earley was in stunning form that day, stronger even than Kelly. Over the second climb just past Aberdalgie he split the field to ribbons and I was at the end of my tether trying to hang on. My cape was flapping in the wind and after four hours of this in the rain I was just about gone. Stockie Muir was the last climb with just over 20 miles to go and my legs were going. I thought there was only one thing for it and that was to ride up near the front and try and look strong, but just then the sprint started for the prime at the top of the hill and I used my last ounce of energy trying to hang on. The run-in was a nightmare. I kept looking at my legs and feeling nothing there and imploring them: 'Just get me to the finish and I promise you a rest'. At the end I was 11 seconds down on Earley. It was a relief in many ways to get out of yellow and away from the pressure but 11 seconds was a lot to make up.

After the Manchester-Liverpool stage which Phil Anderson won I had a go at stealing a few seconds on stage three from Chester to Birmingham, getting in a little move with three laps to go and finally coming fourth in the sprint in a race won by Remig Stumpf of Germany. The Kellogg's was a big breakthrough for Stumpf with three stage wins and a second. I'd always known he was strong but mainly as a lead-out man for others. Here he had never gone so well. Some people say he's the next Bontempi which I think is a bit of an exaggeration. I know I'm faster and can get round him but in the Kellogg's I was never strong enough to get in the right position in the first place. When you start to suffer a bit, someone's past you in a flash. At Cardiff, anyway, I went over Stumpf quite easily.

The crunch of the Kellogg's Tour was always going to be the trip from Birmingham to Cardiff with the First Category climb over the Tumble, a savage, snaking climb above Abergavenny. I knew there was going to be a big shake-up and I knew, too, that I had a fight on to stay where I was in the overall classification. When Bob Millar took off tracked by Nico Verhoeven and Mauro Gianetti it didn't look that serious, but by the top of the Tumble they had 11 minutes and that was it. We chased down the valley into Cardiff but there was nothing we could do about the extraordinary ride by Bob Millar.

Basically the vibes hadn't been right for the whole race but on the last day in Westminster I went out in front to do something, even if it was just to show my face. I knew I wasn't going to stay away and I wasn't really motivated about climbing from fifth to fourth or even third. It was just a case of putting on a bit of a show. I was pleased to see Millar win, more pleased certainly than I'd have been if I'd lost to Earley by a few seconds. In Millar's case it just shows what can be done when there's no pressure on. He had virtually talked himself out of the race and then after one good day he just thought to himself, sod it, I'll go out and give it everything. He had nothing to lose.

12. The Wild Bunch

In France they call it the *peloton*. In Britain it's known as the bunch. Collectively it's the gang of professional cyclists I go to work with on a daily basis, my work-mates if you like, although some are hardly mates. As with any other large group of men there are saints and sinners in the *peloton*. There are guys you could trust with your life and guys you wouldn't turn your back on for a second. There are drinkers and womanisers and even some smokers. Over the years I've made some close friends in there . . . and some enemies.

In some races there are long periods when there's no action and it's quite boring so I have a look round for someone to chat to. Usually it's someone like Johnny Weltz who was with Fagor in 1988, or Neil Stephens, who rides for Paternina. If Deno Davie, the English lad who went to the Italian Carrera team, is there I'll have a good natter with him.

I get on well with Sean Kelly but conversations with him are more on a business level. You can't go up to him and say: 'Did you have a good night last night, Sean?' because he doesn't talk much about things like that. I remember when ANC first went out to the Ruta del Sol, Kelly got on like a house on fire with Phil Thomas. Phil is a very talkative Scouser with an impenetrable accent and he and Kelly were rabbiting away to each other. Nobody could work out what either of them were saying, it was like a foreign language.

Kelly is the riders' rider, if you like, very down to earth and offhand without being aloof. Kelly's a good guy to learn from, too, especially in the hairy bunch sprints. His is a handy wheel to be on if you're jockeying for position because you know he's going to be in the right place at the right time. The trouble is that a lot of other riders know this, too, so there's often a long queue of sprinters behind Kelly, waiting for their chance to go round.

I get on better now with Robert Millar than I did a few years back. At first I really disliked him. In the Tour of Ireland in 1986 Joey was off the front and Millar and his Panasonics were starting to chase. In a situation like that the normal thing to do is to get into their line and try to slow them down so your man in front can get away. Millar came alongside me and said: 'Get out of the way, sonny boy', then he swung across in front of me.

'Do that again and I'll break your nose,' I told him.

So he switched across me again and I took a swing at him, just missing his nose which, let's face it, would be hard to miss!

Millar had a good moan at that and it wasn't a very promising start to a friendship. I didn't get a good impression of him and he certainly didn't like me. Most people don't find him very amenable, but he has mellowed since those days. You can't just talk rubbish to him, you've got to think what you say before you say it because he has a way of making whatever you've come out with sound so utterly stupid. He likes his privacy and a lot of people put that down to ignorance and arrogance. One of his pet hates is people taking photographs of him eating. I don't care for it, either, but Millar goes overboard about it.

Early in the 1988 Tour de France Fagor were sitting in a restaurant when a guy came in and wanted to take a picture of us all at dinner. Often you get television crews in at mealtimes and normally I don't eat while the camera is on me. I just sit there and look at the food. This Spanish photographer said: 'May I take a picture?' Nobody said anything and the guy started fiddling with his camera to set up the shot when a very quiet voice said: 'No.' The guy carried on fiddling and Millar said, a bit louder: 'No.'

The would-be photographer looked up to see if he was joking. Millar slowly stood up, pointed his finger at the door and said: 'Out!'

As a rider, Millar's obviously got a lot of class but he's canny in his use of effort. On days when he does think he can do something you'll never see him – he'll be well up the road.

Sprinters are a select little bunch and at most finishes you find the same guys up there with you. You have to rely a lot on the competence of others if you're racing up a narrow street at 50 miles an hour when a crash could mean serious injury . . . or worse. Sometimes if the racing has been easy during a stage you'll get some people in a bunch sprint who don't belong there, an idiot strain. They try to push and shove and that's when it gets dangerous. Somebody touches a wheel and somebody else brakes and before you know it the whole lot are down. As I say, sprinting is like a club and people who don't belong are always trying to gatecrash. We don't say: 'Oh, you're a climber you can't talk to us, it's sprinters only here', but there is definitely a sort of kinship. Of the sprinters around at the moment the men I rate most are Guido Bontempi of Italy, Mathieu Hermans and Jean-Paul Van Poppel of Holland and Eddy Planckaert of Belgium.

A couple of years back Bontempi was almost untouchable. He didn't look like another cyclist – more like a motor bike in disguise in the bunch. You couldn't ever get round him. Van Poppel is a placid sort of bloke and speaks English and I get on well with him but in the Tour de France he's a killer. He seems to save up all year just for that race. I've had a lot of close finishes with Hermans and you can feel the power coming off him when you're trying to get past. There have been times when I've moved off his wheel and tried to go over him and nothing's happened. He's strong. Planckaert is a really wild finisher probably because he's a Belgian and they don't seem to care whether they live or die! He's very similar to the Kelly of a few years ago – absolutely without fear.

Away from the bunch sprints I get on OK with all of these sprinters. On the flatter days Hermans and Planckaert will sit at the back, ignoring any breaks and we'll have a chat. Hermans speaks good English and so does Planckaert who's quite fluent in Anglo-Saxon, too. He knows all the swear words and uses them!

Cycling is a bit like a freemasonry: it has its secret rites and unwritten rules. If a rider punctures or crashes it's etiquette not to attack him and attacking through the feeding point is supposed to be a bit of a no-no, although when I was with Fagor Valcke was forever getting us to do it and Fignon and his Système-U team are always at it. He would say: 'We'll attack at the first feeding station, so take enough food in your pockets to last all day.' Then when everyone else had taken their musettes and were stuffing their faces we'd hare off up the road. Teka did it in the Tour of Spain in 1989 and that caused a bit of an uproar.

Hand-slinging is supposed to be illegal, too, but sometimes you're sprinting eyeballs out when a guy flies past as if he's jet-propelled and you know a team-mate has grabbed his hand and flung him forwards past you. In the 1989 Milk Race an American was disqualified by the commissaire for putting his hands up on the finishing line. In some situations that can be dangerous. For example, if there's a howling head-wind and you sit back and throw your arms up you can come to a complete stop and the bunch behind could run into you, but that sort of victory salute has become an accepted part of winning and it was ridiculous to penalise one man. As it happened, it was the same commissaire who cost me the yellow jersey in the Sealink International back in April 1982. I had a puncture and he penalised me ten seconds for allegedly being paced back to the bunch by the team car.

There are some real rogues in the *peloton*, too. The Colombians used to have a pretty bad reputation. Any crash and they were automatically blamed for it. I suppose they do fall off a bit more than Europeans and the simple reason is that they just don't concentrate. They are gazing around at the scenery or jabbering away to the bloke behind. It only needs a touch of brakes from someone in front and they're down. Then there are the total prats who are always mouthing off, moaning at people. 'What are you touching your brakes for?' they'll shout at 15 riders in front for slamming on. Nothing's ever right for some of them.

Being professionals, we also have our pride. We don't like being beaten by amateurs, In August 1989, I returned to the track for the first time in four years. It was the Cleveland Grand Prix meeting at Clairville Stadium, Middlesbrough, and I found it hard work getting used to pedalling a lower gear at a tempo and the shorter cranks you need on a track bike. In the final event, the 20 kilometres, I knew I wasn't going to win, so I did all I could to make sure that another professional did.

Tony Doyle and Paul Curran had got away in a break with a local amateur, Andy Chatterton. I knew we could chase them down if we worked hard enough but I wasn't going to chase a fellow pro. Colin Sturgess was thinking the same thing and whenever the bunch began to look dangerous we would go to the front and subtly slow it down a bit to keep Doyle and Curran clear – I knew they'd sort Chatterton out in the sprint. You have to make it look good, though. With about five laps left the break was out of danger so I went on the front and rode a full lap flat-out to keep everyone happy. It was really just to put on a bit of a show because the three who'd got away weren't going to be caught by then. Doyle won the sprint from Curran and professional honour was satisfied.

It's natural instinct. If you're supposed to be in the top class you don't like someone from the lower orders coming along and showing you up, so the pros tend to unite against the common enemy. If that race had been all pros I'd have worked to get the break back and done my best to win, but I wasn't going to tow a load of amateurs around after a fellow professional. It didn't bother me that two or three amateurs went home that night and probably told their mums: 'I beat Malcolm Elliott in a sprint today.' If that is the way they think after beating me for sixth place then they'll always stay amateurs.

Cycling and even cycle training is a dangerous sport and you have to accept that at some stage or other you're going to fall off – or get knocked off – and cut up or injured. I suppose I've been lucky but I've always relied on my instinct for self-preservation to do the right thing and minimise injury. Normally, in a big stack up you are going down with riders who are going at the same speed as you, so you all come down together and injuries aren't that serious. It's when you hit solid objects like cars that you can get badly hurt.

I've seen some pretty bad smashes over the years and the one that springs to mind was in the 1985 Milk Race, coming down a steep hill on the road between Scarborough and Whitby. We were chasing a break and the police had gone ahead and cleared all the traffic off the road. Two Americans with us were doing about 50 down the descent when a car that had been in a filling station pulled out on a blind corner and they hit it head on. I was back down the line and when I went past, a guy called Steve Tilford was stuffed solid in the small space underneath the Ford Escort, motionless. The other rider, Andy Paulin, was 30 yards past the car and its roof had a deep dent where he'd hit it. He was lying in the road and his face was in the tarmac, it looked as though it had been squashed flat. I thought they were both dead. A Czech rider came past me a couple of miles later on in tears. He couldn't believe what he'd seen. We found out later that one had got a broken collar bone and one a broken shoulder and they only spent four days in hospital. I couldn't believe how lightly they got off.

That crash was hard to avoid but the one that put our Teka leader Raimund Dietzen out of the Tour of Spain in 1989 was definitely unnecessary. Two days after my win in Lerida we were finishing a hard climb when we rode into a tunnel. We'd been through a couple of other tunnels that day and they'd rigged 40-watt bulbs every 50 yards, with a generator driving them, but in the last tunnel the generator had failed. There was no lighting at all apart from two motor bikes with lights on stationed at the sides. It was a hell of a long way through and in the middle it was as if you had a bag pulled over your head, we were absolutely blind. The riders were going along calling 'Oh! Oh! Oh!' so that everyone knew where they were but even that was confusing as it echoed off the walls. For those few seconds I was absolutely petrified. Just near the end we came across a crash in the lights of one of the bike headlamps. It was Dietzen looking up the road. He must have touched a wheel and gone straight down.

I went past him – there was nothing I could do and he didn't look too badly injured. It was only when we got back to the team cars after the finish that we heard he'd been airlifted to hospital with a fractured skull. Everyone was staggered. We'd lost our top man because the idiots who ran the Tour had sent us through that tunnel. It could have happened to any one of us and we showed our displeasure by organising a sit-down at the next day's start.

With only the top 18 teams being automatically invited on the 1989 Tour de France, we were aware that it was marginal that we were going to get in anyway, but once we knew Dietzen was away in some hospital bed talking gibberish to himself, that was the final nail in the coffin for Teka and the 1989 Tour. I sat at home and watched it on television although I did get a couple of commentating shifts with Channel Four which I found as nerve-wracking as a bunch sprint!

Alvarino Pino is one of the top riders in Spain but at the time of writing he's an outcast, sent to Coventry by his fellow riders for disobeying one of the sport's unspoken rules. Just after the Tour de France in 1989, there was a minor one-day road race from Zaragoza to Sabiñanigo in Spain. It went up the same climb and into the same tunnel that had wiped out Dietzen in the Vuelta. Amazingly, the tunnel was unlit again and everybody climbed off and refused to go any further. Everyone, that is, except Pino who carried on and rode through to the finish on his own. Even his team were shocked he could do such a thing because the protest wasn't just for the riders that day – it was for Dietzen, too. Even the Spanish riders' union condemned Pino and now he's treated like a leper. And all for coming first in an unimportant race.

You're putting yourself in a dangerous situation just by going out on the road on your bike. Some car-users, of course, think cyclists are there to be shot at. When they gun past and cut you up there's not a lot you can do, although if I get the chance to retaliate I don't hesitate.

I was out training with Micky Morrison once when a GTI-type of car cut us up. I could see the driver looking in the mirror, waiting for my reaction but unfortunately for him he had to stop ahead at some lights and I rode up alongside and just waded in to him, giving him a good hiding. The funny thing was when I'd calmed down, Micky – who's a bit slower to lose his temper – decided to have a go at the passenger and was climbing in on his side. I had to drag him off!

Another time on a training run with some of the lads, some guy we'd had a bust-up with stopped his car in front of a group of us and jumped out wielding a baseball bat. He had to be 'dissuaded' from using it on me.

Mark Walsham was involved in a nasty accident in Sheffield that put him off the road for a time. An old driver in his eighties had cut Mark up on a roundabout and Mark banged on the side of the car and yelled at him. The driver looked out of the window at Mark alongside, whipped his wheel over and bounced Mark right off the road. The police didn't do anything . . . probably because when they arrived Mark had his hands round the old guy's throat!

Sometimes, of course, you finish up in the ditch thanks to a fellow rider. On the 1987 Sun Tour in Australia I had a widely-publicised punch-up with Alessio Di Basco of Italy which finished up with both of us being kicked out of the race.

There was a lot of aggro flying about. Rolf Sorenson of Denmark had to be forcibly restrained from thumping Peter Besanko after the second stage and Walter Brugna of Italy came to blows with Brian Stephens on day five. Brugna was leading at the time and Di Basco had accused me of sitting in behind the Italians, harrassing them. Then on the road from Maffra to Healesville on the seventh day matters came to a head. We'd had a heated discussion when he turned round and rode me into the gravel. I dropped right back then caught him up again. I was just about to tell him to put up or shut up when he reached across and whipped my handlebars away. I went sprawling. I climbed back on, fuming, and chased after him, but every time I tried to get past to land him one he just wheeled me across the road. We were dropping further and further behind the bunch as I tried to get up to chin him and eventually the race referee pulled alongside and disqualified us both.

The Sun Tour's a good place for fisticuffs. In 1985 I was there in a composite team along with Steve Jones and Philippe Lauraire, a very good French sprinter. Both of them got away in a break and the Spanish were chasing and I got in among them to slow them down. One of them bawled: 'Get out of it!' and gave me a shove. I got back to him and said: 'If you've got something to say to me, say it at the finish' and then forgot all about it. He hadn't, though, because at the finish he came over and started again. We squared up. People started gathering to see the fun, and fists started flying. Mine was the only one that made contact – just once – before they pulled us apart. I still see this Spaniard, Manol Murga, now and we have a good laugh about it, but Di Basco has always stayed in my 'little black book'.

Another name in that book is the Russian, Abdujaporov, who is still the most aggressively lethal rider I've ever come across, definitely the biggest lunatic I've seen on two wheels. In the 1986 Milk Race he rubbed everyone up the wrong way and, given half the chance, I'd have had him off. What's more I'd have made sure he couldn't get up again because there's no point in knocking him off just so he can get back up and do the same to you.

One group of people a professional rider must rely on, if he's to stay upright, is the team mechanics. When my tyre rolled off in York that was down to a careless mechanic who'd stuck it on the rim without enough care. That's a sobering thought when you're throwing the bike into corners down some Alpine hairpin.

I've become used to checking most things myself. I'm probably more exacting than a lot of other riders. The mechanics think, 'Oh, here he is again, what is it now?' If I don't find something I'm unhappy about, then they think there's something wrong and may suggest: 'Your brakes must need centring or something. How about your tyres, do you want some more air in them?' They're baffled if I don't go and pester them. But I don't want to get on my bike, start a stage and five miles into it see the wheel rubbing on the brake. I feel more calm before the start if I know everything is perfect. I'm not saying I'm better than the mechanics but they have nine bikes on a team to look at and only a certain amount of time to spend on each, so they can overlook things. My life's on the line so I've got to be sure.

A cyclist can do everything right in his career but one thing he can never take account of is the weather. On a bike you do see the extremes and most of the extremes are in the Tour de France.

On stage 15 of the 1987 Tour from Tarbes to Blagnac the heavens opened halfway through and the rain came bucketing down. I don't think I've seen anything like that before or since. The rain got heavier and heavier. In one town there had been a flash flood and we turned this corner and almost disappeared underwater. It was up to the bottom brackets on the bike and I thought, Christ! If I stop here I'll never get going again . . . I'll just drown. Then we got to a hill and I thought it would ease off but there was a river, two feet deep, running down it. The day before that the tarmac had been melting in the heat!

Some of the mountain stages in the Tour are horrendous. I don't go badly in the heat but if you're going uphill and there's no fresh breeze around, it can be like riding inside a furnace.

The worst race for cold, surprisingly, was the 1986 Sun Tour when a lot of riders finished up with hypothermia. We were in the Victorian Alps, on Mount St Bernard, and there was a 20-kilometre climb to a ski station. It had started to rain in the valley and as we got higher the rain turned to sleet and the sleet turned to snow until we found ourselves in the middle of a blizzard. For about ten kilometres we were riding in five inches of snow, trying to get in the wheel tracks of the cars in front. None of us had legwarmers and the thing that probably saved me from frostbite or worse was that as it was the last race of the season I hadn't shaved my legs. I had a fair bit of hair growing on them and these hairs just froze into lumps which acted as a sort of insulation.

I remember Neil Stephens won the stage and at the finish he cycled straight over to his brother who was standing by the line. His hands were so cold he held them out to his brother and told him: 'Pee on my hands.' Some riders were in a right state after that race, coming in 15 or 20 minutes down. That was a great finale to the season!

Every rider has his own idea about how to spend the winter and how to train off the bike. There's probably an ideal way and then there's my way! I look on winter as the one opportunity to spend a bit of time as a normal human being, whereas someone like Kelly will probably try and stay completely dedicated 52 weeks of the year. He will probably put his bike away at the end of the season and then start running every day, whereas I will try a few different things to keep a semblance of fitness. I might do a bit of running off the road and a light weights programme. The idea is to find something that's hard enough to be of benefit to you but that you'll enjoy too. The problem with weights or circuit training is that it has to be hard to be any good, so the place I come to hate is the gym. I actually start looking forward to the start of the season to get out of it.

The Continental professionals don't go in for weights as much and as they have the best record, perhaps they are right. In Europe they like runnning, a bit of squash and some skiing. A lot of the French teams have a winter training camp which is fairly regimented. I've never ski-ed, so it wouldn't suit me. It would just be a waste, stumbling around for a week, trying to get some semblance of balance and direction.

On Sundays I'll go out on the bike with the lads, doing about 50 or 60 miles with lunch at a pub and a few beers. Sometimes that can get a bit over the top, like the time we rode over from Sheffield to the Snake Inn, had five or six pints, then decided to carry the bikes over to Edale across the 2,000-foot Bleaklow plateau. It's hard work walking uphill in cycling shoes with a racing bike over your shoulder but by then we were past caring!

From January it's up from one to two or three rides a week of at least two or three hours, trying to get drawn into a few little burn-ups and preparing myself for the fact that in a month's time I'm going to be doing it for real. When the season does start it's a horrible feeling looking round in that first race and believing that everyone else is fitter than you, but the thing is to go into it and try not to let it knock you to pieces. You've probably got another 129 races to go in that year!

At 28, I figure on another five years in top class racing. It depends how long I can keep the mental interest going because physically there should be no problem. A sprinter is what I am and what I've become but there's no reason why I can't improve my all-round ability, become a bit stronger. I can't see myself slowing down but as you get older you can win races on experience rather than speed, like Wise Old Kelly. Perhaps one day it will be Wise Old Elliott. After that I'd like to get involved in a team, an English team, as manager. It would be nice to stay involved with the big race atmosphere but without the pain. Perhaps one day the riders will be slagging me off behind my back, but they're welcome to do that. I know, better than most, that they'll have earned that right.

Career Record

1977   Silver medal, national schoolboys circuit race
        championship

1978   North Midlands Division BCF junior road race
        champion

1979   North Midlands Division junior road race
        champion
        1st, Ronde Anglia (counting event for Peter
        Buckley Trophy)
        1st, West Common road race (counting event for
        Peter Buckley Trophy)
        Joint 2nd overall, Peter Buckley Trophy
        37 wins as a junior
        Became senior in July and won five road races in 13
        days
        1st, Star Cycle League
        Represented Britain in pursuit and road race at
        world junior championships in Argentina

1980   Based for four months in France, scoring four wins
        1st, Stannington Trophy road race, Sheffield
        1st, National Hill-climb championship, Nick O'
        Pendle
        3rd, stage 1, Sealink International, Hook of
        Holland

Member of the GB 4,000 metres pursuit team at Moscow Olympic Games with Tony Doyle, Sean Yates and Glenn Mitchell. The team qualified 5th fastest, briefly holding the Olympic record, before being eliminated in quarter-finals by Czechoslovakia

1981   Awarded Sebastian Coe Trophy for outstanding contribution to sport by Sheffield citizen

1982   1st, Commonwealth Games road race, Brisbane, Australia
1st, Commonwealth Games team time trial, Brisbane
Hot-spot sprints winner, Milk Race
3rd overall, Sealink International

1983   1st, prologue time trial, plus five stage wins, Milk Race
3rd overall, Milk Race
1st, prologue, Sealink International
1st, Lincoln Grand Prix Star Trophy race
1st, Roevin Grand Prix, Hyde
1st, Tour of the Peak
1st overall, Star Trophy
1st, Kettering International Criterium
3rd overall, three day Circuit of the Ardennes, France

1984   PROFESSIONAL Raleigh-Weinmann
1st overall, Sealink International
1st, national criterium championship, Birmingham
3rd, national road race championship
1st, stage 1, Penn two-day, Wolverhampton
1st, Anglia TV race, Norwich
1st, Sheffield City Centre race
1st, time trial stage, Ron Kitching Great Yorkshire Classic
1st, Kellogg's City Centre race, Nottingham
1st, Milton Keynes Bowl GP

1985   Raleigh-Weinmann
1st, British pursuit championship
1st, Sun Tour, Australia
1st, round two, Michelin Grand Prix series
1st, Barnsley Town Race
1st, Ron Kitching Criterium, Harrogate
1st, Cleveland Criterium
1st, Brighton Criterium
1st, Milton Keynes Criterium
1st, Ever Ready road race, Wolverhampton
3rd overall, Kellogg's City Centre series

1986   ANC-Halfords
1st, stage 3, Milk Race
1st, stage 9, Milk Race
2nd overall, Milk Race
1st, stage 6, Sun Tour, Australia
1st, stage 16, Sun Tour
3rd overall, Sun Tour
1st, Eastway Criterium
1st, Peel Criterium, Isle of Man
1st, Dublin Kellogg's City Centre race
1st, Shaw Town race
3rd, Grand Prix d'Albacete, Spain

1987   ANC-Halfords
1st, prologue, Milk Race
1st, stage 1, Milk Race
1st, stage 2, Milk Race
1st, stage 3, Milk Race
1st, stage 6, Milk Race
1st overall, Milk Race
1st overall, Tour of Lancashire
1st, stage 1, Nissan Classic, Ireland
1st, stage 4, Nissan Classic
1st, stage 5, Nissan Classic
1st, stage 4, Sun Tour, Australia
3rd, Amstel Gold Race, Holland

3rd, stage 12, Tour de France
2nd overall, Kellogg's Tour of Britain

1988   Fagor
1st, prologue, Kellogg's Tour of Britain
1st, stage 1, Kellogg's Tour of Britain
1st overall, Kellogg's Tour of Britain
1st, stage 17, Tour of Spain
1st, stage 3, Tour of Aragon, Spain
1st, stage 14, Sun Tour, Australia
2nd overall, Nissan Classic, Ireland
4th, final stage, Tour de France
1st, Kellogg's City Centre race, Cork

1989   Teka
1st, stage 3, Tour of Spain
1st, stage 11, Tour of Spain
1st overall, on points, Tour of Spain
1st, prologue, Semaine Catalan, Spain
1st, stage 1, Semaine Catalan
1st, stage 2, Trophy Castilla Leon, Spain
1st, stage 4, Trophy Castilla Leon
1st, Tour of North East Derbyshire
1st, stage 2, Tour of Galicia, Spain
1st overall, on points, Tour of Galicia
1st, prologue, Kellogg's Tour of Britain
5th overall, Kellogg's Tour of Britain
2nd, stage 7, Tour of the Americas
2nd overall, Tour of the Americas